Sunday Dinner
in the South

OTHER BOOKS
BY TAMMY ALGOOD

Farm Fresh Southern Cooking

In a Snap!

The Southern Slow Cooker Bible

Sunday Dinner in the South

Recipes to Keep Them Coming Back for More

Tammy Algood

NELSON
BOOKS
An Imprint of Thomas Nelson

Published in Nashville, Tennessee, by Nelson Books, an imprint of Thomas Nelson. Nelson Books and Thomas Nelson are registered trademarks of HarperCollins Christian Publishing, Inc.

Photography by Mark Boughton

Food and prop styling by Teresa Blackburn

Thomas Nelson titles may be purchased in bulk for educational, business, fund-raising, or sales promotional use. For information, please e-mail SpecialMarkets@ThomasNelson.com.

Image on page 56 © Shutterstock.com/Robyn Mackenzie

Image on page 100 © Shutterstock.com/sarsmis

Image on page 156 © photodisc

Photos © 2015 Thomas Nelson

Library of Congress Cataloging-in-Publication Data

Algood, Tammy.
  Sunday dinner in the South : recipes to keep them coming back for more / Tammy Algood, Tammy Algood.
      pages cm
  Includes index.
  Summary: "Food personality Tammy Algood shares more than 180 recipes for Southern comfort food, combined with forty funny and heartwarming stories from preachers about Sunday dinners in the home of church members.Delving deep into the South's romance with dinnertime after church ;Sunday Dinner in the South serves up the recipes and stories of Southern pastors who have enjoyed the hospitality of parishioners for generations. Weaving together the South's two greatest traditions;cooking and storytelling;Algood brings readers to the Sunday table of Southern homes.;And while Sunday dinner is often the most indulgent meal of the week, Algood devotes a portion of the book to recipes for health-conscious readers. Dishes such as Spicy Sweet Potato Soup with Greens, Fresh Corn Polenta with Cherry Tomatoes, and Roasted Brisket with Country Vegetables will inspire readers to preserve and continue the grand tradition of Southern Sunday dinner"-- Provided by publisher.
  ISBN 978-1-4016-0539-1 (hardback)
1. Cooking, American—Southern style. 2. Cooking—Religious aspects. 3. Dinners and dining—Southern States—Anecdotes. 4. Southern States—Social life and customs. I. Algood, Tammy. II. Title.
  TX715.2.S68A394 2015
  641.5975—dc23
                                                                              2014037713

Printed in China

19 20 21 22 23 DSC 7 6 5 4 3 2

With love and gratitude to my husband, George, who
holds my heart and makes me laugh!

Contents

Introduction

When is dinner? In the South, it's the midday meal that some call lunch. It's not to be confused with the evening meal, which is called supper. I still have a hard time calling it anything else and love the revival of supper clubs that are keeping the word alive.

Unlike any other day of the week, an old-fashioned Sunday dinner is reserved for nothing less than feasting. You might make do the rest of the time, but on Sunday, cooks across the South will pull out all the stops. And that's especially true if the local preacher is going to be attending the meal served at your home after church. The acceptance of that invitation is a reason to really put on a show and have a dining table loaded with abundance.

The slightly chipped, well-loved serving bowls on this day are usually filled with items from the garden, and this is the case no matter what time of year it happens to be. That's because Southern cooks have a long tradition of "putting up food," and pantries are typically filled with jars of green beans, corn, squash, tomatoes, soups, jams, and everything else that was harvested during the growing season. But the centerpiece is usually a meat that requires the home's largest platter to present it well on the recently starched and ironed tablecloth.

That's the traditional dinner for the local pastor, preacher, brother, rabbi, father, priest, or bishop. However, these days that meal might be very different from those served in the past. While the leader of your church is most concerned about spiritual health, physical health is certainly not a neglected part of ministry. So seasonal eating with lighter fare is very much appreciated by clergy of all ages and all denominations. That lends itself to serving economical soups, sandwiches, and salads to curb the appetites of hungry guests and family members while the main meal is being prepared in the kitchen or out on the grill, or to serve as the meal itself. With that in mind, you'll find an entire chapter dedicated to these types of dishes that are designed to be easily prepared, easy on the budget, and quick to work off in the gym.

Today, dinner might be served buffet-style over family-style, depending on the size of the dinner table and the number of people seated there. The fact is, there is only one rule: no one lifts a fork until the preacher or patriarch of the family says the blessing, which is commonly referred to as "returning thanks" or "saying grace" in the South. The hungrier you are, the longer that prayer might seem, especially if the fried chicken is anywhere close to your seat at the table!

Even the conversation at Sunday dinner is different from any other mealtime talk. It mainly focuses on the food itself, with accolades and compliments galore. And of course the exchange will include many references to the fine sermon that morning. It would be downright rude to bring up anything controversial! Only joy and the music of silverware clanking against the treasured family china are allowed to be a part of this feast.

It always amazed me how my own mother could attend church with all of us in tow and somehow have an incredible dinner on the table after we returned home in practically no time flat. By the time we could get ourselves changed out of our "Sunday go to meetin' clothes" and into our play clothes, she would have a much anticipated, incredible meal waiting for us to devour. I still don't know how she managed to do it. My very favorite meal was her exceptional Chicken Spaghetti (page 158), which I still make to this day and think of her every time it is served.

This cookbook is a collection of memories just like that—where one dish stands out among the many offered on the most sacred of days and the most cherished of all weekly meals. It honors those who feed us spiritually from the pulpit and those who do the same for our physical needs from the kitchen. As long as there is a South, there will be a showcase of memorable culinary excellence on display each Sunday that is ready to be enjoyed as soon as "Amen!" is uttered! May your own family dinners be blessed by these heartwarming stories and these Sunday dinner–worthy recipes.

Fresh Tomato Tartlets (page 23)

Appetizers

White Pimento Cheese

While some think of pimento cheese as a sandwich spread, true Southerners know it's also a side dish or an appetizer served with crackers. This version is designed not to compete with the yellow cheese that often accompanies macaroni or steamed broccoli. It is exceptional served over hot baked potatoes or stuffed in pods of pickled okra.

YIELD: 3 CUPS

1 (8-ounce) package cream
   cheese, softened

1/2 heaping cup small-curd
   cottage cheese

1 1/2 cups shredded white
   Cheddar cheese

1 (4-ounce) jar diced pimientos,
   drained

1 1/2 teaspoons honey mustard

1 1/2 teaspoons mayonnaise

1/4 teaspoon onion or garlic salt

1/4 teaspoon hot sauce

1/4 teaspoon white pepper

1 tablespoon coarsely chopped,
   toasted pecans or walnuts for
   garnish

Place the cream cheese and cottage cheese in the bowl of a food processor and puree until smooth. Transfer to a medium bowl and stir in the white Cheddar, pimientos, honey mustard, mayonnaise, onion salt, hot sauce, and white pepper. Cover and refrigerate at least 2 hours. When ready to serve, garnish with the pecans. Serve cold.

NOTE: *Refrigerate leftovers and use within 3 days.*

SERVING SUGGESTION: *If you would like to serve this as a cheese ball, increase the amount of white Cheddar to 2 cups and roll into a large ball before refrigerating. Finely chop the pecans and mix with 2 tablespoons of chopped fresh parsley. Roll the ball in the pecan and parsley mixture and serve cold with assorted crackers.*

Slow-Cooked Broccoli Dip

On chilly days, you need something to warm dinner guests upon arrival. This does so without spoiling appetites for the meal to come. Plus, you can start it before you leave for church and it's ready when you return.

YIELD: 16 SERVINGS

....

2 (10.5-ounce) cans cream of celery or cream of mushroom soup

2 (10-ounce) packages frozen chopped broccoli

1 (8-ounce) jar sliced mushrooms, drained

1 (8-ounce) package cream cheese, softened

1/2 (12-ounce) package frozen chopped onions

1 (4-ounce) package goat cheese

1 (4-ounce) package slivered almonds

1/2 teaspoon garlic salt

1/4 teaspoon black pepper

Bagel chips

....

Lightly grease a small or medium slow cooker. Place the cans of soup, broccoli, mushrooms, cream cheese, onions, goat cheese, almonds, garlic salt, and pepper in the cooker. Cover and cook on the low setting for 4 hours or until melted. Stir well before serving warm with chips.

NOTE: *This dip can be left uncovered for serving in your slow cooker on the warm setting for up to 1 1/2 hours. Stir frequently.*

SUNDAY DINNER MEMORIES

Meals are always best when shared, and Sundays tend to put us in a different frame of mind from any other day of the week. It's a more reflective day and perfect for breaking bread together. That's part of the reason the Reverend Molly Dale Smith started the Sunday Supper Club at Saint David's Episcopal Church in Nashville, Tennessee.

As the priest associate, she realized the need for merging education and food. She began the club in the fall of 2011 in order to combine food with the education programs to draw folks into the event and provide a sense of community. It is still going strong as a monthly organized potluck because her instincts were right on target.

Although Molly was born in New York, she has deep Southern roots that drew her family back to Nashville when she was in the eighth grade. She understands the almost visceral connection that Southerners have to hospitality and the lovely gift it is to others.

The Sunday club is designed to address a program topic for discussion, but it's centered around fellowship. It is beautifully fluid to meet the spiritual and financial needs of the attendees. If you want to cook, great! Bring a dish of your choosing. If you would rather not, that's not a problem because there are other ways to contribute. That might be helping clean up, rearranging the chairs, or washing the dishes. Everyone is always welcome at Saint David's.

Molly is still salivating over their most recent meal, which included a juicy meatloaf, creamy mashed potatoes, cooked-just-right green beans, tangy lemon bars, gooey brownies, and delicious wine. While each of the food items could not stand alone as a complete meal, together they were perfection.

And that's the way it is with the group. Once a month, by being together, they enhance each other. They are an ever-expanding family of believers who have transformed a potluck into a monthly celebration of God's abundance.

Pea and Bean Cracker Spread

I love this spread on low-salt crackers, but don't limit its use there. It's also terrific with celery and carrot sticks, and leftovers can serve as a sandwich spread instead of mayonnaise. It keeps well in either the freezer or the refrigerator.

Yield: 3 cups

2 cups frozen English peas, thawed

2 cups frozen baby lima beans, thawed

2 large garlic cloves, peeled and minced

3 tablespoons olive oil

1 tablespoon lemon juice

1/2 cup crumbled feta cheese

1/2 teaspoon onion salt

1/4 teaspoon black pepper

Paprika

Assorted crackers

Place the peas, beans, garlic, olive oil, lemon juice, feta, onion salt, and pepper in the bowl of a food processor. Process until smooth. Transfer to a serving bowl and sprinkle with paprika. Serve immediately with assorted crackers, or cover and refrigerate for up to one week.

NOTE: *You can substitute crumbled blue cheese for the feta if desired.*

Herb Garden of Eden Cheese

This is a great way to use up fresh herbs, especially during the last weeks of summer when you can't seem to clip enough to keep the plants under control. Spread some of this cheese under the loosened skin of a chicken and roast for a creamy, luscious entrée.

YIELD: 2 CUPS

2 (8-ounce) packages cream cheese, softened

1/2 cup half-and-half or milk

2 garlic cloves, peeled and minced

2 tablespoons chopped fresh parsley

2 tablespoons chopped fresh chives

1 tablespoon chopped fresh basil

1 tablespoon chopped fresh thyme

1/4 teaspoon onion salt

1/4 teaspoon black pepper

1/8 teaspoon cayenne pepper

1/8 teaspoon paprika

In a medium bowl beat the cream cheese with an electric mixer on medium speed until creamy, about 2 minutes. Add the half-and-half, garlic, parsley, chives, basil, thyme, onion salt, black pepper, cayenne, and paprika. Blend on low speed until well mixed and smooth, about 2 minutes.

Refrigerate at least 2 hours before serving. To freeze: After the mixture is cold, divide and shape into 2 logs. Wrap in plastic and place in a heavy-duty zip-top freezer bag. Freeze up to 6 weeks. Thaw overnight in the refrigerator. Serve with assorted crackers.

SUNDAY DINNER MEMORIES

Age is definitely a state of mind, and Reginald Johnson, at ninety, is proof of that. Now retired after over forty years in the Lutheran church, Reg, as his friends call him, is living in Atlanta, Georgia, and still swims at least twice a week.

He spent the majority of his ministry in Virginia, but grew up in Kentucky and "cut his teeth" there in the few Lutheran churches that dotted the landscape at the time.

Reg is a fan of almost all types of Southern cuisine. He grew up poor and was thankful for what was in front of him on the table. If he had to select favorites, it would be fried pork chops, crowder peas, and chess pie. But Reg proudly says, "I'm like an old goat. I will eat anything!"

It was in the hills of Kentucky where he had his most memorable meal at the home of Jake and Betsy Fuller. Both were proud, hard-working parishioners who rarely missed church. There were many times when they weren't properly dressed for the service, but they came anyway and were always polite, quiet, and appreciative of any kindness that came their way.

It was a crisp, fall day when Reg decided to drop by their modest home and pay a visit. "I really wasn't planning on it, but just happened to be near their home and decided to stop in," Reg recalls.

As he entered their property, chickens scattered and a hound dog barked to signal that someone was there, but Reg couldn't find Jake or Betsy anywhere. He was leaving when he met the couple headed down the drive with loaded cloth sacks in their arms. After a proper greeting, Betsy said they were just coming in from work to have a picnic and that Reg must join them.

"She was already pulling a blanket out of one of the sacks and spreading it when she asked me," he recalls. The picnic consisted of sliced apples, some leftover bread, and fresh lemonade. And it was perfectly simple, deliciously filling, and "just enough" to make the walk back home pleasant.

Reg declares that he was taught a valuable lesson that day, and it has stayed with him his whole life. The true meaning of God's provision is that there is abundance in scarcity.

Peach and Lady Pea Salsa

This recipe does double duty. It can be a way to tame hunger while you are putting the last-minute touches on dinner, or you can use it as a topping for roasted or grilled meat or fish. Feel free to substitute any leftover cooked peas you have for the lady peas in this unique blend of sweet and savory.

YIELD: 4 CUPS

....

1 large fresh peach, peeled, pitted, and diced

2 jalapeño peppers, seeded and minced

3 tablespoons lime juice

1 tablespoon sugar

2 teaspoons orange zest

2 cups cooked lady peas

1/3 cup finely chopped red onions

1/2 cup chopped fresh cilantro

....

In a medium bowl gently stir together the peaches, jalapeños, lime juice, sugar, orange zest, peas, onions, and cilantro. Cover and refrigerate at least 8 hours and up to 24 hours. Serve with blue corn chips or over grilled chicken.

NOTE: *You can substitute nectarines or apricots for the peaches if desired.*

Sunday Dinner Memories

In the twenty years Willie McLaurin has been in ministry, he has been asked to bless a lot of food, and Willie has prayed over the aromas of many Southern specialties. He is particularly grateful to have his head bowed over personal favorites of country fried steak, sweet potato casserole, and piping-hot wedges of buttered cornbread.

Like all of us, he has distinct food preferences when it comes to Sunday dinner. Waldorf salad gets a thumbs-up, while cheesecake made from a box doesn't rate very high in the enthusiasm department.

In addition to being on staff at the Tennessee Baptist Convention, he is the interim pastor at the First Baptist Church in McEwen, Tennessee. On a recent brisk November day, he headed to dinner with a family who had relocated from Louisiana to Tennessee.

This meal was different from the beginning. For starters, the hosts prepared the meal after Willie arrived, so it was quite literally fresh off the stove when served. Then he experienced something that could only be described as a divine plate of New Orleans cuisine. He enjoyed a feast of Chicken Bienville on angel hair pasta, perfectly seasoned garlic bread, and a fresh garden salad.

The meal was so special to him that he obtained the recipe from the family who so lovingly prepared it for his dinner. Now the same meal has continued to bless his own family and friends.

Mary's house. Joe still recalls how even though he was just this young intern, she acted like she was having lunch with the king of England that day.

. . .

Today, Joe has moved well beyond that internship and serves as the head of staff at a two-hundred-year-old church in Columbia, Tennessee. But Mary's grace-filled display of genuine appreciation brings a tender smile to his face even now as he remembers how he dined with Southern royalty.

Creamy Jalapeño Spinach Dip (page 22) with Herbed Homemade Crackers

Herbed Homemade Crackers

These addictive homemade crackers are a cinch to prepare. You'll have a sturdier cracker with the wrappers and a more delicate one with the dough, so select according to your preference. I keep a batch on hand at all times. Serve these alone or with any local cheese and pear slices.

YIELD: 40 CRACKERS

....

4 tablespoons butter, melted, divided

20 wonton wrappers, eggroll wrappers, or phyllo dough

I tablespoon chopped fresh chives

I teaspoon salt, optional

....

Preheat the oven to 375 degrees. Brush 1 tablespoon of the melted butter on two baking sheets.

Cut each of the wrappers or phyllo dough diagonally into 2 triangles. Place close together on the prepared baking sheets. Brush the tops with the remaining 3 tablespoons of melted butter.

In a small bowl combine the chives and salt and sprinkle evenly over the dough. Bake 5 minutes or until lightly browned. Transfer to a cooling rack and serve warm or at room temperature.

NOTE: *Store leftovers in an airtight container at room temperature for up to 10 days.*

Barbecued Chicken Meatballs

I love meatballs, but quickly tire of the same ones made with beef. This lighter version is a nice change of pace and not as heavy or filling.

YIELD: 14 SERVINGS

---

1 large egg

1 (2-pound) package ground chicken

1 cup dry seasoned bread crumbs

2 tablespoons chopped fresh parsley

2 tablespoons chopped fresh cilantro

1 teaspoon garlic or onion salt

1 (16-ounce) bottle barbecue sauce

Whisk the egg in a medium bowl and stir in the chicken, bread crumbs, parsley, cilantro, and salt. Cover and refrigerate 30 minutes.

Preheat the oven to 375 degrees. Lightly grease 2 rimmed baking sheets and 2 wire cooling racks. Place the cooling racks on the rimmed baking sheets. Using a large scoop or your hands, shape the chicken mixture into 1-inch balls and place on the racks. Bake 20 minutes.

SERVING SUGGESTION #1: *Transfer the cooked meatballs to a lightly greased small slow cooker and turn on warm or low heat. Cover with the barbecue sauce and serve warm with picks.*

SERVING SUGGESTION #2: *Transfer the cooked meatballs to a warm serving platter and drizzle with the barbecue sauce. Place the remaining sauce in a bowl and serve with the meatballs for dipping.*

NOTE: *Leftovers freeze well. Package, label, and freeze, then use within 3 months for the best quality.*

Wild Mushroom and Goat Cheese Salsa

I love unusual salsa recipes and after sampling something similar during a weekend trip to Georgia, I developed this version. It certainly cannot be accused of being subtle, and that's the whole point!

YIELD: 2 CUPS

....

2 tablespoons canola
  or vegetable oil

1 tablespoon butter

4 green onions, thinly sliced

1 (12-ounce) package wild
  mushrooms, chopped

2 garlic cloves, peeled and
  minced

1/4 cup low-sodium vegetable
  stock

1 tablespoon low-sodium soy
  sauce

1 (10-ounce) package crumbled
  goat cheese, softened

1/2 cup chopped pecans or
  walnuts, toasted

2 tablespoons chopped fresh
  parsley

1 teaspoon chopped fresh thyme

1 teaspoon grated lemon zest

1/2 teaspoon onion salt

1/4 teaspoon black pepper

1/8 teaspoon cayenne pepper

Toasted crostini or bagel
  crackers

....

Place the oil and butter in a large skillet over medium heat. When the butter has melted, add the onions and mushrooms. Sauté 5 minutes, then add the garlic, stock, and soy sauce. Sauté 5 minutes longer.

In a serving bowl stir together the goat cheese, pecans, parsley, thyme, lemon zest, onion salt, black pepper, and cayenne. Add the warm mushroom mixture and stir well to combine. Serve immediately or cover and refrigerate until ready to serve with crackers.

NOTE: *Leftovers can store up to 3 days tightly covered in the refrigerator.*

Creamy Jalapeño Spinach Dip

After a summer of growing hot peppers, I spent lots of time dreaming of ways to use them without overpowering the rest of the dish. I really appreciate the heat on the back end of this dip that makes it pair well with any crackers, especially the Herbed Homemade Crackers (page 19) made with wonton wrappers.

YIELD: 10 SERVINGS

---

2 tablespoons canola or
    vegetable oil

2 large jalapeño peppers, seeded
    and minced

2 pimientos or mild peppers,
    minced

1 sweet onion, peeled and
    chopped

1 (14-ounce) can diced tomatoes,
    undrained

1 (8-ounce) package cream
    cheese, cut in pieces and
    softened

1 tablespoon white wine vinegar

1 (10-ounce) package frozen
    chopped spinach, thawed and
    squeezed dry

3 cups shredded Monterey Jack
    cheese

1 cup half-and-half or milk

1/2 teaspoon garlic salt

Preheat the oven to 350 degrees. Lightly grease an 11 x 7-inch baking dish.

Place the oil in a large skillet over medium-high heat. Add the jalapeños, pimientos, and onions. Sauté 5 minutes and stir in the tomatoes and their juices. Bring to a boil and cook 3 minutes.

Add the cream cheese and white wine vinegar, stirring until the cheese has completely melted. Add the spinach, Monterey Jack cheese, half-and-half, and garlic salt, stirring to blend. Transfer to the prepared baking dish and bake 30 minutes. Serve warm.

NOTE: *Leftovers can be gently reheated on low power in the microwave.*

Fresh Tomato Tartlets

Phyllo cups make quick work of this appetizer that can be assembled in a flash. Toss the tomato mixture together ahead of time, and you've got a meal starter that looks complicated but isn't! Leftover tomato filling goes great on a green salad, baked potato, rice, grits, an omelet, or as a pasta topper. (Photo on page xii.)

YIELD: 6 SERVINGS

---

2 cups small grape or cherry tomatoes, cut in half lengthwise

3 garlic cloves, peeled and minced

2 tablespoons chopped fresh basil

1 tablespoon chopped fresh oregano

1 tablespoon chopped fresh parsley

2 tablespoons red wine vinegar

2 tablespoons extra-virgin olive oil

1 teaspoon kosher salt

1/4 teaspoon black pepper

1 (1.9-ounce) package frozen phyllo cups, thawed

1/4 cup crumbled feta cheese

Place the tomatoes in a medium bowl. Sprinkle evenly with the garlic, basil, oregano, parsley, red wine vinegar, olive oil, salt, and pepper. Toss lightly and let stand at room temperature at least 1 hour before using.

Toss the tomato mixture again and spoon into the phyllo cups. Garnish with the feta and serve immediately.

NOTE: *The tomato mixture can be prepared ahead of time and refrigerated. Bring to room temperature at least 30 minutes before using.*

Salads

Springtime Salad with Almonds

When Southern yards and gardens wake up after a long winter's nap, you'll find all kinds of culinary delights to be carried into the kitchen. It becomes a bit of a daily surprise to see what is ready to be harvested. This salad is not only beautiful but tastes like spring. Gone are the heavy salads and dressings of winter. It's time to lighten up!

YIELD: 6 SIDE SERVINGS

3 tablespoons olive oil

I tablespoon red or white wine vinegar

I tablespoon lemon juice

1/2 teaspoon seasoned salt

1/4 teaspoon black pepper

3 cups spring salad mix

I cup baby arugula

I carrot, peeled and cut into ribbons

6 radishes, trimmed and cut into thin wedges

1/3 cup slivered almonds

2 tablespoons shaved Parmesan cheese

In a jar with a tight-fitting lid, combine the olive oil, vinegar, lemon juice, seasoned salt, and pepper. Shake to emulsify.

Place the spring mix and arugula in a large salad bowl and toss gently with the dressing. Evenly divide among 6 salad plates and distribute the carrots, radishes, and almonds on top. Garnish with the Parmesan and serve immediately.

NOTE: *Use a vegetable peeler to cut the carrot into ribbons.*

Sunday Dinner Memories

Tammy Wright grew up on a farm in the east Tennessee town of Maryville. She was living in Madisonville and had a family with three small children when she realized God was calling her into ministry.

She quickly found out that the University of the South in Sewanee, Tennessee, was going to accept Methodist students even though it was an Episcopal seminary. They had already accepted twenty-four students and had slots for twenty-five. Within days, Tammy had sent her college transcripts, references, and letters from pastors recommending her. By the end of that week, she was notified that she was accepted as the twenty-fifth student. It was simply meant to be, and proof that God works in mysterious ways. Today, she is the pastor of Jonesborough United Methodist Church and is right at home in Washington County.

Her current church family loves having potluck meals after Sunday services. They have come to realize it is a great way to fellowship and welcome newcomers to their community. With everyone contributing to the meal and cleanup, it's easy and economical for everyone and has evolved into a much-anticipated social event.

One of the dishes Tammy likes to take is a seven-layer salad because she can make it ahead of time. Before one potluck event, Tammy found that she didn't have enough time to fry the pound of bacon called for in the recipe. So she went to the supermarket and grabbed a container of already cooked bacon pieces that could simply be sprinkled on that layer of the salad. It turned out beautifully with plenty of time to spare! *Why didn't I think of this before now?* was her thought at her stroke of brilliance.

During the potluck, Tammy heard a parishioner say, "Who made this seven-layer salad?" to which Tammy proudly took credit. It was lovely, after all. About that time, the man bit into the oxygen-absorber packet that was in the package of bacon bits! Tammy's heart felt like it was going to stop.

"When he pulled that packet out of his mouth, I just could have died," Tammy explains. "Yes, we all ended up laughing about it for quite some time. It is still a big joke to this day, but it is also the last time I ever tried to take that particular recipe shortcut!"

Unclouded Day Sunshine Salad

I am always looking for sun in any form during the winter season. This salad is like a cloudless day on a dinner plate. It utilizes everything that winter showcases in the produce department, which keeps it low in cost but elegant. Add roasted chicken or turkey to make it a complete meal.

YIELD: 6 SIDE SERVINGS

---

3 tablespoons olive oil

2 tablespoons lemon juice

2 tablespoons Dijon mustard

1 tablespoon white wine vinegar

1/2 teaspoon salt

1/4 teaspoon black pepper

1 head Bibb lettuce, washed and torn

2 oranges, peeled and divided into sections

1 pink grapefruit, peeled and divided into sections

1/4 cup sliced almonds

Place the olive oil, lemon juice, Dijon, white wine vinegar, salt, and pepper in a jar with a tight-fitting lid. Shake to emulsify.

Place the lettuce, oranges, and grapefruit sections in a large salad bowl and toss with the dressing. Garnish with the almonds and serve immediately.

NOTE: *The dressing can be made ahead of time and kept refrigerated, but separation will occur. Shake well to emulsify before using.*

Cool Breeze Poppy Seed Fruit Salad

Seeing this salad on the plate is an instant feast for the eyes. My husband says it's like a nice, cool breeze on a melting hot summer day. I couldn't agree more.

YIELD: 6 SERVINGS

....

1/2 cup cider vinegar

I cup sugar

2 tablespoons poppy seeds

I teaspoon dry mustard

I teaspoon onion salt

I cup canola or vegetable oil

Mixed salad greens

2 large sliced seedless watermelon, cut into bite-size chunks

I cantaloupe, cut in half, seeded and scooped with a small melon baller

I (2-pound) fresh pineapple, cored, peeled, and cut into bite-size chunks

I quart fresh strawberries, capped and sliced

I 1/3 cups fresh blueberries

....

Place the cider vinegar, sugar, poppy seeds, dry mustard, and onion salt in the bowl of a food processor and blend. With the motor running, add the oil in a slow, steady stream through the shoot until the dressing is emulsified.

Place the mixed greens on cold salad plates and top evenly with the watermelon, cantaloupe, pineapple, strawberries, and blueberries. Drizzle with the dressing and serve immediately.

NOTE: *The dressing can be made ahead of time and kept refrigerated, but separation will occur. Shake well to emulsify before using.*

Cool as a Cucumber Soup (page 34)

Soups

Cool as a Cucumber Soup

It took me awhile to warm up to the notion of cold soups, but I am a true fan now. This one is a perfect meal starter during the hot summer months. Serve it in small cups or glasses. I love that it can be made ahead of time and served straight from the fridge. (Photo on page 32.)

YIELD: 6 TO 8 SMALL SERVINGS

2 tablespoons olive oil

2 garlic cloves, peeled and minced

2 1/2 pounds (8 medium) tomatoes, peeled, seeded, and chopped

1/2 teaspoon onion salt

1/4 teaspoon black pepper

2 large cucumbers, peeled, seeded, and chopped

1/2 cup tomato juice

1 1/2 tablespoons red wine vinegar

1/4 teaspoon hot sauce

Minced fresh chives for garnish

Place the olive oil in a large skillet over medium heat. Add the garlic and sauté 1 minute. Stir in the tomatoes, onion salt, and pepper and cook another 5 minutes, stirring frequently. Remove the pan from the heat to cool at least 10 minutes.

Place the cucumbers in the bowl of a large food processor or blender and puree. Add the cooled tomato mixture, tomato juice, red wine vinegar, and hot sauce. Puree until smooth, adding more tomato juice if necessary for a soup-like consistency. Transfer to a large bowl and cover. Refrigerate at least 4 hours. Serve cold with a garnish of minced fresh chives.

NOTE: *Refrigerated leftovers should be used within 2 days.*

Hearty Sausage and Bean Soup

This soup can be assembled ahead of time and cooked as soon as you get home. Within forty-five minutes, you've got dinner ready, which gives you just enough time to bake some cornbread and serve it alongside the soup in sliced buttered wedges.

Yield: 10 servings

I pound ground hot or mild pork sausage

I sweet onion, peeled and chopped

I cup diced carrots

I cup diced celery

3 (14-ounce) cans low-sodium chicken stock

2 (14.5-ounce) cans diced tomatoes with basil, oregano, and garlic

2 (16-ounce) cans dark-red kidney beans, drained and rinsed

I (16-ounce) can light-red kidney beans, drained and rinsed

2 cups ditalini pasta*

I teaspoon garlic salt

I teaspoon black pepper

Fresh chopped parsley for garnish

In a large Dutch oven over medium-high heat, cook the sausage, onions, carrots, and celery for 7 minutes. Drain the grease and add the stock, tomatoes, and kidney beans. Bring to a boil, then reduce the heat to medium-low and simmer 20 minutes. Add the pasta and cook 9 minutes longer. Stir in the garlic salt and pepper and serve warm with a garnish of fresh parsley.

* Ditalini is tiny, short, tube-shaped pasta. Feel free to substitute orzo if you wish.

Sunday Dinner Memories

As a Catholic priest, Father Raymond Jones was used to a regimented system of order and structure. It provided him comfort, and he relished it in his church and in his life. By his own admission, it made his world easy.

Every Tuesday he went to visit patients in the hospital around his parish in New Orleans. He would arrive around nine in the morning and stay until the job was done, and he always had a pimento cheese sandwich in the cafeteria at lunch. Some days took longer than others, but he welcomed the opportunity to help those in physical pain. One of those visits in the summer of 2006 provided him with his most memorable meal.

It was already stifling hot when Raymond arrived at the hospital, and he knew it was only going to get worse as the day progressed. The air was still, and nothing seemed to be moving other than the steady stream of cars bringing visitors and employees to the hospital.

By now, he was a recognized figure at the facility, so he made his way through the halls and corridors with ease, stopping to greet the nurses and doctors as he passed. At noon, he was perched on his usual chair, about to enjoy his pimento cheese sandwich.

It was then that he noticed what looked like a college-aged young man sitting over to the side staring into space. Raymond went over to him and gently asked if he would like some company. The young man just looked at him and said nothing.

Coconut Chicken Soup

The secret to getting this soup on the table in a hurry is to prep and measure the ingredients ahead of time. The coconut milk gives it a nice, sweet surprise. Fish sauce can be found in the Asian area of your supermarket.

YIELD: **8** SERVINGS

4 cups water

3 cups fresh spinach leaves

1/2 pound snow peas, cut in half crosswise

1 (5.5-ounce) package plain ramen noodles

1 tablespoon canola oil

2 large shallots, peeled and chopped

1 1/2 teaspoons curry powder

1/2 teaspoon ground turmeric

1/2 teaspoon ground coriander

2 garlic cloves, peeled and minced

6 cups low-sodium chicken stock

1 (13.5-ounce) can light coconut milk

2 1/2 cups coarsely chopped cooked chicken

1/2 cup chopped green onions

2 tablespoons sugar

2 tablespoons fish or low-sodium soy sauce

1/2 cup chopped fresh cilantro

1/4 teaspoon crushed red pepper flakes

1 lime, cut into 8 wedges for garnish

Place the water in a large saucepot over medium-high heat. Bring to a boil and add the spinach and peas. Cook 30 seconds and remove from the cooking water with a large slotted spoon. Place in a large serving bowl. Add the noodles to the water and cook 2 minutes. Drain and add the noodles to the spinach bowl.

Return the pan to the stove, still over medium-high heat, and add the oil. When hot, add the shallots, curry powder, turmeric, coriander, and garlic. Sauté 1 minute, stirring constantly. Add the stock and bring to a boil. Stir in the coconut milk and reduce the heat to low. Simmer 5 minutes. Add the chicken, onions, sugar, and fish sauce. Cook 2 minutes and pour over the noodle mixture. Stir in the cilantro and red pepper flakes. Ladle into warmed bowls and serve with a lime wedge for garnish.

NOTE : *You can substitute pork or turkey for the chicken.*

Sunday Dinner Memories

Jackson, Mississippi, was a big small town when Arnold Burgess moved there in the early 1970s. He had taken a job with the Church of Christ right out of seminary. It was just the kind of place he had hoped for, and he was anxious to prove himself worthy of the associate position.

It wasn't long before he came to know Katherine Curtis and her mother, Mary Alice. Katherine was a widow, and not long after her husband died, Mary Alice came to live with her. Arnold remembered thinking at the time how nice it was, but also knew the situation must have its challenges.

He received very little mail at the time, and was pleasantly surprised when he received a handwritten invitation to join them for soup the following Sunday for dinner.

He arrived that Sunday after church with some hand-picked daisies and instantly felt at home. Mary Alice was sitting outside under a large oak tree, and Arnold joined her. They were in the middle of a lovely conversation when Katherine came out carrying cups of artichoke soup on a large tray. "We sat under that tree and sipped on the best soup I have ever tasted," he recalls. "I didn't even know what an artichoke was, but the soup was divine!"

The afternoon breeze kept them cool, and it seemed to be time to leave sooner than Arnold wanted. Near the end of the visit, he commented on how he admired the way they were able to live so well together and be a source of support to each other. Katherine said that at first she dreaded the arrival of her mother into her home. But after adjusting, she was grateful for the time she had been given with her.

Mary Alice added that her goal was to always remember that it was Katherine's home. She knew that when her daughter had lived with her, she was in charge; but it was the opposite now, and she tried to keep that in mind. Arnold said those words have been put to good use as he is now living in his daughter's home. And he is grateful that he heard the sermon preached over cups of soup that Sunday.

Church Ran Long Spring Pea and Ham Soup

Occasionally it takes a bit longer to get home from Sunday services and you have a famished family on your hands. This recipe can be made on the spot. Small cups of this refreshing soup can be served as a first course or a warm appetizer. Or load up hefty mugs and accompany it with a fresh green salad and crusty bread for a full meal.

YIELD: 4 TO 6 SERVINGS

2 teaspoons olive oil

2 leeks, trimmed and diced

2 (19-ounce) cans ready-to-serve split pea with bacon soup

1 1/2 cups apple juice

2 medium carrots, peeled and chopped

1 cup cooked, diced ham

1/2 teaspoon black pepper

Place the olive oil in a large saucepan over medium heat. When hot, add the leeks and cook 3 minutes or until just tender. With a slotted spoon, remove the leeks and place on paper towels to drain.

Add the soup, apple juice, carrots, ham, and pepper to the saucepan and bring to a boil over medium heat. Reduce the heat to low, cover, and simmer for 15 minutes or until the carrots are tender. Ladle warm soup into bowls and top with the reserved leeks.

NOTE: *Refrigerated leftovers should be used within 3 days.*

Pumpkin Seed and Tomatillo Gazpacho

Husk tomatoes or tomatillos are grown all over the South, and you'll find loads of them in farmers' markets beginning in mid-summer. Pair them with crunchy pumpkin seeds and you've got a unique make-ahead meal that's a real stand out.

YIELD: 8 SERVINGS

1/2 heaping cup unsalted and shelled pumpkin seeds

2 pounds tomatillos, husked and rinsed

1 large poblano pepper

1 garlic clove

1 cup low-sodium chicken or vegetable stock

1/2 teaspoon salt

1/4 teaspoon black pepper

1/3 cup chopped green onions

1/4 cup chopped fresh cilantro

1/4 cup olive oil

1 small cucumber, diced

1 avocado, peeled, pitted, and diced

1 (12-ounce) container cherry tomatoes, halved

Prepare the grill to medium-high heat. Finely grind the pumpkin seeds in the bowl of a food processor. Leave them in the processor and set aside.

Grill the tomatillos and poblano pepper until the tomatillos are slightly charred and the pepper is charred all over, around 13 to 15 minutes. Add the tomatillos to the food processor. Peel, seed, and coarsely chop the pepper and add to the food processor, along with the garlic. Process until coarsely pureed and transfer to a large bowl. Stir in the stock, salt, and pepper. Cover and chill about 3 hours until cold. Just before serving, stir in the onions, cilantro, olive oil, cucumbers, avocadoes, and tomatoes. Serve cold or at room temperature.

NOTE: *This soup freezes well. Package, label, and freeze, then use within 2 months for the best quality. To liven it up a bit after being frozen, squeeze a wedge of fresh lime into the mixture.*

SUNDAY DINNER MEMORIES

Every November you can count on Thanksgiving week to rank as the most heavily traveled time of the year. Countless folks juggle plans in order to be home for the holiday that is uniquely American. It is the one day dedicated solely to the harvest and the seasonal foods that are gifts to each of us. It is a special time to return thanks to the Giver.

Thanksgiving Day of 1980 ended up giving Sally Hughes many reasons to be grateful. As pastor of the Historic Franklin Presbyterian Church in Franklin, Tennessee, she underlines the importance of family and gratitude constantly. But as a young seminary student in Richmond, Virginia, Sally found herself far from home and bound by time constraints that would not allow her to return for Thanksgiving.

She wasn't alone as there were another dozen or so students who were also "homeless" for the holidays. Rather than marinate in the circumstance, they all decided they would enjoy the day together. After choosing a place to gather, the apartment of one friend that was large enough to accommodate the entire bunch, plans were set in motion.

Each person or couple was assigned to bring some dish that represented home to them. On Thanksgiving Day, there was plenty of wine and a long table full of foods that reflected the best of each person's traditional family Thanksgiving dinner.

After they were all seated and before the meal was blessed, someone said, "Wow, we are just like grown-ups!" And while the room erupted in laughter, it was the exact moment when they all realized it was true. They had crossed the threshold into the real grown-up world, and there was no turning back.

For Sally, that fantastic meal on that glorious day has held a special place in her heart. The preparations that had to be made and coordinated for that meal underlined for her the same work her mother and grandmother had done for years. As a child, she came bounding to the table when everyone said it was ready. As a grown-up, she saw that large gatherings for a meal of any kind don't just happen. Behind the scenes, there are many puzzle pieces that have to come together to make the complete picture. It's the often unrecognized gift you give to those you have over for dinner, and while it may be missed by some, it's not overlooked by Sally.

Mississippi Spinach Soup with Roasted Pears

I experienced a version of this soup at a restaurant in Corinth, Mississippi, and have finally come close to replicating it. It is totally habit forming and can become a meal quickly if you don't limit the portion sizes. Otherwise, guests will continue to go back for more until it is gone! It can be made ahead to the point of pureeing. Gently reheat and continue as directed when adding the cream and butter.

YIELD: 8 SERVINGS

8 ripe pears, peeled, cored, and cut into 1-inch slices

4 tablespoons olive oil, divided

1 large sweet onion, peeled and chopped

2 garlic cloves, peeled and minced

6 zucchini, chopped

2 cups apple cider or apple juice

8 cups low-sodium chicken stock

1 (10-ounce) package fresh baby spinach

1/4 cup pear butter*

2 tablespoons lemon juice

1 tablespoon honey

1 teaspoon Worcestershire sauce

1/2 teaspoon garlic or onion salt

1/2 teaspoon dry mustard

1/2 teaspoon ground cinnamon

1/4 teaspoon black pepper

1/4 teaspoon white pepper

1/8 teaspoon ground ginger

4 cups heavy cream or half-and-half, divided

4 tablespoons butter, cut in pieces

Preheat the oven to 400 degrees and grease a baking sheet. Add the pears and toss with 2 tablespoons of the olive oil. Spread in an even layer and roast 20 minutes. Let cool 5 minutes.

Add the remaining 2 tablespoons oil to a Dutch oven and place over medium heat. Stir in the pears, onions, and garlic and cook, stirring frequently, for 8 minutes. Add the zucchini and cook 12 minutes longer. Add the cider and scrape any stuck pieces with a wooden spoon. Add the stock and bring to a simmer.

Stir in the spinach, pear butter, lemon juice, honey, Worcestershire, garlic salt, dry mustard, cinnamon, black pepper, white pepper, and ginger. Cover and reduce the heat to low. Simmer for 1 hour.

With an immersion blender, puree the soup until smooth. Add 3 3/4 cups of the cream and stir until completely combined. Remove from the heat and whisk in the butter until melted. Serve with a drizzle of the remaining 1/4 cup cream as a garnish.

* If you can't locate pear butter at your supermarket, substitute apple or peach butter.

Sunday Dinner Memories

I thought I would go into ministry for just a little while," admits Harry Morton, "and I never left. I remember thinking that my life as a pastor would be temporary, but I was with the Church of Christ for nearly forty-five years."

A remarkable life experience was the outcome, and Harry wouldn't trade a moment of it. Now that he is retired and living in sunny south Florida, he cannot imagine what other path he could have walked. Along that journey came some exceptional meals that ranged from large and extravagant to intimate and simple. Admittedly, he has eaten foods he never imagined consuming under the guise of being polite and has become the better man for it.

One such occasion happened at the home of Phyllis and Mark Thomas, who eventually became treasured friends. When they first met, the couple had just relocated to Florida from Arkansas. Harry was amazed at how quickly they settled into their new home, and when he paid the first visit, it seemed as if they had been living there for decades.

It wasn't long before they invited Harry to one of their summer barbecues, and it led to other frequent invitations of Sunday dinners. Harry always enjoyed the gatherings as well as meeting the wide range of neighbors who inevitably were on the guest list.

At one particular dinner, he was told the meal was going to be soup, Caesar salad, and French bread. Since Phyllis was an exceptional cook, Harry looked forward to it, and the intoxicating aromas met him at the door. After mingling a bit, it was time to sit down and partake of the meal spread before them. That's when Harry heard Phyllis say that the main course was turtle soup.

Although Harry had never tasted turtle soup, the thought of it made his stomach turn. But as he had learned to do, he was going to make the best of this situation and give it a try. "On numerous attempts, I nearly got the spoon to my lips," he recalls, "but I just couldn't put it in my mouth for some reason and kept putting the spoon down."

Everyone else was raving about the meal while Harry concentrated on his salad and bread. He kept trying to eat the soup, only to fail each time. When Phyllis left the table to get more bread, Mark quickly switched his empty bowl with Harry's full one. He never said a word, but just took care of it silently and efficiently. "I'm sure the look of appreciation on my face said it all," Harry remembers, "and I suddenly realized what a great friend he was. Phyllis never knew, and it ended up being one of the best times I ever had with the two of them."

Baby Bella Mushroom Soup

When making mushroom soup, it's important to use mushrooms that are full of flavor. Baby bellas are just the pick and give great depth to this vegetarian soup.

YIELD: 10 SERVINGS

1 large sweet onion, peeled and chopped

4 garlic cloves, peeled and minced

6 tablespoons butter

2 (16-ounce) packages baby bella or brown mushrooms, chopped

2 tablespoons paprika

6 tablespoons all-purpose flour

8 cups low-sodium vegetable stock, divided

4 cups milk

1/2 cup chopped fresh parsley

1/2 teaspoon celery salt

1/4 teaspoon black pepper

1/8 teaspoon cayenne pepper

Fresh chopped chives for garnish

In a large Dutch oven over medium heat, combine the onions, garlic, and butter. Cook 7 minutes, stirring frequently. Add the mushrooms and continue cooking for 10 minutes. Add the paprika and flour and cook 5 minutes longer.

Gradually add 4 cups of the stock and the milk. Increase the heat to medium-high and bring to a boil, stirring frequently. Add the remaining 4 cups stock, parsley, celery salt, black pepper, and cayenne. Cover and remove from the heat. Let stand 5 minutes and serve warm with a garnish of fresh chives.

NOTE: *This soup freezes well. Package, label, and freeze, then use within 2 months for the best quality.*

Down-Home Lentil and Fresh Vegetable Soup

Even if you don't have time to garden, you can enjoy a great soup by utilizing the wide variety of vegetable options on the market. This one celebrates the most common vegetables pulled from Southern gardens.

YIELD: 6 TO 8 SERVINGS

3 cups water

2 1/2 cups low-sodium vegetable or chicken stock

1 sweet onion, peeled and diced

2 celery stalks, sliced

2 small parsnips, peeled and sliced

2 cups fresh corn

1 cup sliced fresh mushrooms

1 cup dried lentils

3 tomatoes, peeled and diced

1 tablespoon fresh chopped parsley

1 teaspoon garlic salt

1 medium zucchini, cut in half lengthwise and sliced

In a large Dutch oven over medium-high heat, combine the water, stock, onions, celery, parsnips, corn, mushrooms, lentils, tomatoes, parsley, and garlic salt. Bring to a boil and reduce the heat to medium-low. Cover and simmer for 35 minutes, stirring occasionally. Stir in the zucchini, cover, and simmer 25 minutes longer. Serve warm.

NOTE: *You can substitute large carrots for the parsnips if desired.*

Sandwiches

Lamb and Goat Cheese Burgers

Ground lamb is such a nice switch from a traditional beef burger. Use goat cheese from local sources and fresh cilantro from your herb garden to make this meal memorable. The burgers can be formed up to a day in advance, then refrigerated and grilled later.

YIELD: 6 SERVINGS

3 pounds ground lamb

2 large eggs

1/4 cup Worcestershire sauce

1/4 cup chopped fresh cilantro

1 teaspoon garlic powder

1 teaspoon black pepper

6 ounces goat cheese, sliced

6 hamburger buns

1/4 cup mayonnaise

6 lettuce leaves

6 tomato slices

6 onion slices

Preheat the grill to medium-high. In a large bowl combine the lamb, eggs, Worcestershire, cilantro, garlic powder, and pepper. Form the mixture into 6 patties and transfer to the grill. Cook 5 to 6 minutes on each side, then place on a serving platter. Top immediately with the goat cheese and let rest 3 minutes.

Spread each bun with the mayonnaise and divide the lettuce, tomatoes, and onions among the buns. Top with the burgers and serve warm.

NOTE: *After the burgers are formed, make indentions in the top with your fingers. This helps prevent the meat from buckling at the top as it cooks.*

Hot Turkey Sandwich with Avocado Mayonnaise

I became a fan of sprouts years ago after numerous trips to farmers' markets. I avoided purchasing them for a while, but when I did I was surprised they had tons of flavor. Here they match well with moist turkey and a creamy avocado mayonnaise that has a bit of kick.

YIELD: 6 SERVINGS

1 large avocado, peeled and seeded

3/4 cup mayonnaise

1 jalapeño pepper, seeded and finely chopped

2 tablespoons chopped fresh cilantro

1 tablespoon lime juice

1/2 teaspoon onion salt

1/4 teaspoon white pepper

6 split rolls or toasted bread slices

1 (16-ounce) package smoked turkey slices

10 ounces alfalfa or bean sprouts

6 tomato slices

6 Swiss or Provolone cheese slices

Place the avocados, mayonnaise, jalapeños, cilantro, lime juice, onion salt, and white pepper in the bowl of a food processor and process until smooth. Liberally spread the avocado mayonnaise mixture over each piece of bread. Top evenly with the turkey, sprouts, tomatoes, and cheese. Cut each sandwich in half and serve immediately.

NOTE: *Use sprouts quickly, within 2 days of purchasing if possible. Keep them in the refrigerator crisper drawer in the ventilated package you bought them in.*

SUNDAY DINNER MEMORIES

Ted Roman is a retired pastor who is ninety-one years old and still as active as can be. He is a darling mixture of sass and brass that endears anyone who has the honor of spending time with him.

Ted preached with fervor for fifty-two years after receiving the calling late in life at the age of thirty. In his words, "I had an inkling about becoming a pastor my whole life, but kept pushing the thought aside until it finally caught up with me." From that moment forward, he made up for lost time, moving as a Methodist minister in churches throughout the Carolinas.

His most cherished Sunday meal was in the home of Abigail Rockwood, who was a music teacher and church pianist. "That woman put fear into the hearts of many, and I was one of them. Sing off-key or miss a chord and you would be sorry," he explained.

Abigail caught Ted off guard one Sunday when she *told* him he would be having dinner with her right after the service. And while Ted didn't necessarily want to go, he had no excuse, so off he went to Abigail's home when the last of the attendees had left the sanctuary.

Ted really didn't know what to expect, but he had a feeling the meal would be very formal. To his amazement, she had prepared simple tomato sandwiches that they ate on well-loved, chipped dishes on the screened-in porch. She explained that she had a tomato sandwich every Sunday after church because it was her deceased husband's favorite meal. Ted's first thought was, *What? Abigail Rockwood used to be married?* Evidently her husband always told her she made the best tomato sandwiches in the whole world. All of a sudden Ted had a new appreciation for Abigail. Those tomato sandwiches were her way of honoring her husband and keeping his memory a part of her life. Ted and Abigail enjoyed a great friendship after that day, and guess what Ted has for dinner every Sunday after church?

Spiced Black Bean and Cheese Sliders

I love sliders, those miniature versions of hefty burgers. They are exceptional at a midday meal when you've likely got things to accomplish in the afternoon. I prepared these for my most devoted meat-loving friends and they were hooked. You will be too!

YIELD: 5 SERVINGS

4 1/4 cups cooked black beans, well drained

6 button mushrooms, cut in half

1 carrot, peeled and coarsely chopped

2 garlic cloves, peeled and minced

1 small jalapeño pepper, seeded and coarsely chopped

2 large eggs

1/4 cup half-and-half

2 teaspoons chili powder

1 teaspoon onion salt

1/4 teaspoon black pepper

3–4 cups panko or dry plain bread crumbs*

1/4 cup vegetable oil

10 small rolls

1/4 cup prepared guacamole

5 slices Provolone cheese, cut in half

In the bowl of a food processor, place the beans, mushrooms, carrots, garlic, jalapeños, eggs, half-and-half, chili powder, onion salt, and pepper. Puree until smooth. Transfer to a large bowl and gently fold in the bread crumbs. Let stand for 15 minutes.

Place the oil in a large cast-iron skillet over medium-high heat. Divide the bean mixture into 10 portions and shape into patties. Fry 2 minutes on each side in the skillet. Work in batches and drain on paper towels.

To serve, spread the split rolls with the guacamole. Place half of a Provolone slice on each roll half. Top with the warm patty and serve warm.

NOTE: *If guacamole is not to your liking, use a flavored mayonnaise instead.*

* Play with the amount. You want the burgers to hold together but not be too dry.

SUNDAY DINNER MEMORIES

Walter Bryant spends a lot of his time remembering. Although he is physically confined to a wheelchair, his mind is free to roam the memories of his blessed life. He devoted fifty-six years of it to ministry, beginning as a missionary and morphing into leadership in the Baptist church.

No matter where he went, his best friend, Tom, was always a phone call away, so it thrilled the both of them when they were able to take weeklong fishing trips together each spring and fall. "We fished everywhere," Walter remembers, "and often brought along our grandchildren to share the experience."

It was one of those occasions when Tom brought along his grandson Jimmy, who was six years old at the time. Jimmy was a precocious little ball of energy similar to a worm in hot ashes—he was never still for a moment. Getting him to remain calm on the fishing boat was their biggest challenge, but that task was instantly accomplished when Jimmy caught his first fish. From then on, he was still as a statue while waiting for the line to dip.

Packing the picnic lunch was always Walter's job, but Jimmy begged to make it for their outing the last day. Naturally, Walter gave in to him. Jimmy wanted it to be a surprise, so while Walter and Tom readied the equipment, he made lunch. Walter had given him the cooler with ice packs already in the bottom, so all Jimmy had to do was load the cooler and they were set for a day of fun.

The morning was fantastic, with each catching their fair share of the bounty. Jimmy talked all morning about how much they were going to love the lunch he made. Finally the time came to pull ashore, stretch their legs, and unpack the much-anticipated lunch. Jimmy did the honors, and the men were surprised that he had carefully wrapped each sandwich in aluminum foil just as Walter had usually done. After blessing the food, it was time to unwrap the sandwiches, and Jimmy insisted they close their eyes to take the first bite.

The taste was unusual to both friends, but familiar. Jimmy had made them mayonnaise sandwiches! The pride on his face kept them from voicing anything but praise. And as they sat by the water's edge, they had the most pleasant lunch they had ever experienced. Jimmy called them his "Magic Sandwiches," and indeed they were.

Potato Chip Chicken and White Cheddar Sandwich

Instead of having chips on the side, they add to the salty crunch of this sandwich. It works best with thin potato chips rather than corn chips, and I like plain rather than flavored thanks to the spices added in the mix.

Yield: 4 servings

Vegetable oil

1 (14.5-ounce) bag potato chips

1 teaspoon ground coriander

1 teaspoon paprika

1 teaspoon black pepper

4 large eggs

1 cup all-purpose flour

4 boneless skinless chicken breasts, pounded to a 1/2-inch thickness

4 tablespoons mayonnaise

4 hamburger buns or split rolls

4 lettuce leaves

4 slices white Cheddar or Provolone cheese

Place a half inch of oil in a large cast-iron skillet and set over medium-high heat. Open the potato chip bag and add the coriander, paprika, and pepper. Crush the chips and transfer the crumbs to a shallow dish.

Place the eggs in a separate shallow dish and the flour in a third shallow dish. Dip the chicken first in the flour, shaking to remove the excess, and then the eggs. Finally, dip in the potato chip mixture, making sure to press well to evenly coat. Fry in batches for 5 minutes on each side and drain on paper towels.

To assemble the sandwiches, spread the mayonnaise evenly on the buns. Top with the lettuce and cheese, then the chicken patties. Cut in half and serve warm.

NOTE: *Crisp up leftovers in a preheated 400-degree oven for 8 minutes.*

Pecan Salmon Croquettes with Lemon Butter

What could be better than fried pecan-crusted salmon? Not much, and you can prepare the patties ahead of time and keep them refrigerated until ready to fry. The lemon butter is nothing short of remarkable.

YIELD: 4 SERVINGS

2 to 4 tablespoons vegetable oil, divided

1 (12-ounce) can pink salmon, drained and flaked

2 large eggs

1 large shallot, peeled and chopped

1 slice white bread, finely crumbled

2 tablespoons cornmeal

2 tablespoons mayonnaise

1 teaspoon Worcestershire sauce

1 teaspoon hot sauce

1/2 teaspoon garlic salt

1/2 teaspoon black pepper

3 tablespoons all-purpose flour

1/2 cup finely chopped pecans

6 tablespoons butter, softened

1 tablespoon lemon juice

1 tablespoon chopped fresh parsley

Toasted bread slices

Place 2 tablespoons of the oil in a large skillet over medium heat. In a large bowl combine the salmon, eggs, shallots, bread crumbs, cornmeal, mayonnaise, Worcestershire, hot sauce, garlic salt, and pepper. Gently combine, and if the mixture is too moist, add the flour a tablespoon at a time to adjust the consistency.

Divide the mixture into 4 equal portions and form into patties. Press each side into the pecans and fry two at a time in the hot oil about 4 minutes per side, turning only once. Drain on paper towels and add more oil to the skillet if necessary. Repeat with the remaining patties.

Combine the butter, lemon juice, and parsley in a small bowl. Spread evenly on the bread slices. Add the salmon patties and serve warm.

SUNDAY DINNER MEMORIES

It takes a lot of energy to go on a vacation. You have to plan, pack, unpack, and hope it turns out to be relaxing. Martin Reynolds decided that when he retired from ministry with the Episcopal church, he would become an exceptional tourist. Getting away from it all was his new passion.

Off he went to destinations he never had time for while he was a priest. Europe, Australia, and Canada were at the top of his list, and after a couple of years, he decided to take a break so he could get his mother's house in Lexington, Kentucky, ready to sell.

So with the same zest he had for planning trips to lands far away, he settled himself into the job of taking care of the business at hand. After a few weeks, he decided to take a few days off and reconnect with friends. They planned to meet after church at a "meat and three" that was convenient and close by. Martin arrived just as his other friends were parking and was surprised they were able to park so close to the restaurant. They soon realized why when they saw the establishment was closed. Since there was a small sandwich shop next door, they decided to eat there instead and quickly found a booth near the front.

They ordered from the ordinary menu, with none of them expecting much since their hopes had been pinned on the other restaurant. After all, how exciting could a ham and cheese sandwich with plain potato chips be?

The friends quickly caught up while waiting for their food, and before too long, they had steaming sandwiches in front of them. Martin was pleasantly surprised because he, along with his friends, expected the sandwiches to be cold. Then, as each took a bite, groans of meal pleasure began. "Honestly, it was the best sandwich I ever had!" Martin recalled. "The bread was soft and fresh, the ham was slightly sweet, the cheese had a bit of punch to it, and chopped black olives were sprinkled over the healthy smear of mayonnaise," he added.

As he returned to his household chores, he reflected on that tiny sandwich shop and went back to it on a regular basis. By the time the house sold, he was a regular customer and realized he was truly going to miss eating there. It was then that he understood he no longer wanted to be a tourist; he wanted to be a traveler. He wanted to really get to know the places he was visiting, not just see the sights, and find the treasures that he knew awaited him if he got off the beaten path. He is grateful that a warm ham and cheese sandwich taught him that lesson!

Quick Dinner Rolls (page 78)

Breads

Jalapeño Cornbread Biscotti

Think of this bread as a giant flavor-filled crouton. It adds crunch to soups and salads and keeps well for snacks during the week that follows. You can easily substitute a milder pepper for the hot version called for in this recipe.

Yield: 15 pieces

2 (6-ounce) packages buttermilk cornbread mix

1 cup shredded pepper jack cheese, divided

2 large jalapeño peppers, seeded and minced

4 tablespoons butter, cut into pieces

3 large eggs, divided

1/4 cup buttermilk

Preheat the oven to 350 degrees. Line a baking sheet with parchment paper and lightly grease.

In the bowl of a food processor, combine the cornbread mix, 3/4 cup of the pepper jack, and jalapeños. Add the butter and pulse 5 times until crumbly.

In a medium bowl whisk together 2 of the eggs and the buttermilk. With the processor running, gradually add the egg mixture through the chute and process until well moistened. Spread the thick batter onto the prepared baking sheet using lightly greased hands.

In a small bowl whisk the remaining egg and brush over the top of the batter. Sprinkle evenly with the remaining 1/4 cup cheese.

Bake for 20 minutes or until pale brown. Let cool on the baking sheet on a wire rack for 10 minutes and reduce the oven temperature to 300 degrees.

Slide the loaf onto a cutting board and cut into 1/2-inch diagonal slices with a serrated knife. Place a new piece of parchment on the baking sheet and place the slices flat. Bake 15 to 17 minutes on each side or until golden and crisp. Cool on the baking sheet on a wire rack for 15 minutes. Serve warm.

NOTE: *The prepared biscotti can be frozen up to 2 weeks if necessary.*

Tomato Cheese Bread

This delicious bread can be made in a hurry and utilizes the tomatoes and basil from your summer garden. It pairs well with any simple green salad, white chili, buttered noodles, or homemade soup.

Yield: 4 servings

4 (1/2-inch thick) slices Italian bread

1 tablespoon butter, softened

1 tablespoon Dijon mustard

4 (1-ounce) slices mozzarella cheese

1 large tomato, peeled and sliced into 4 thick pieces

1/4 small sweet onion, thinly sliced

1 tablespoon chopped fresh basil

1 teaspoon freshly ground black pepper

Preheat the broiler to high and lightly grease a baking sheet. Place the bread slices on the prepared sheet and broil 30 seconds on each side to lightly toast. Remove the bread from the oven and immediately brush one side of each slice with butter, then with the Dijon. Top with the mozzarella, tomato slices, and onions. Sprinkle evenly with the basil and pepper. Broil 2 minutes longer and serve warm.

Cornmeal Biscuits

These buttermilk biscuits have just a little bit of what I call "umph" to hold up to meals that feature pork chops or fried chicken. But they are also fantastic holders of butter and homemade jam if you want to serve breakfast for dinner.

YIELD: 8 SERVINGS

3 cups all-purpose flour

1/2 cup plus 1 teaspoon self-rising cornmeal, divided

6 tablespoons cold butter, divided

1/4 cup vegetable shortening, cut into pieces

1 1/2 cups buttermilk

In a large bowl stir together the flour and 1/2 cup of the cornmeal. Cut in 4 tablespoons of the cold butter and the shortening with a pastry blender or 2 forks until the dough is crumbly. Cover and refrigerate 10 minutes.

Preheat the oven to 500 degrees and sprinkle the remaining 1 teaspoon of cornmeal on an ungreased rimmed baking sheet. Melt the remaining 2 tablespoons of butter in a glass dish in the microwave on low power for 20 seconds and stir until melted.

Make a well in the center of the flour mixture and add the buttermilk, stirring just until moistened. Turn the dough out onto a floured surface and knead 4 times. Roll the dough into a 3/4-inch thick circle.

Cut the dough with a 2-inch cutter, rerolling the scraps as needed. Place the cut biscuits on the prepared baking sheet. Brush the tops with the melted butter and bake 13 to 15 minutes or until golden brown. Serve warm.

NOTE: *These biscuits cook marvelously on cast iron.*

Sunday Dinner Memories

Rarely do teenagers realize what they were placed on earth to do, but that's not the case for Devin Pickard. At only seventeen years old, he began preaching and has continued to this day. Now the preacher at Fairfield Church of Christ in Centerville, Tennessee, he remains in the ministry where he was called to nearly thirty years ago.

Throughout that time frame, Devin has enjoyed many meals expertly prepared and served in the homes of his congregation. He is particularly drawn to desserts and is insanely partial to caramel pie and peanut butter cake. When asked to single out an especially memorable experience, he doesn't hesitate. It is any meal at the table of his most beloved parishioner . . . his mom.

Devin knows that he will always be in for a surprise when he has dinner at his mother's home. That's because Debbie Pickard understands the true meaning of spirit-filled hospitality. She opens her home to anyone who happens to be traveling through town with a genuine kindness that makes them feel like family.

Oma is what everyone calls Debbie now, thanks to lovely grandchildren who are the only ones with the power to change adults' names. Oma is always quick with an invitation to those who are visiting the church, wanting them to feel the embrace of the community long after Devin has finished the sermon. "She's such a great example of grace and giving," Devin says, and in her actions there is a great lesson.

"I remember once when these strangers stayed at the house a couple of days because they were looking for work," Devin recalls. "She cared for them and fed them like they were royalty!" At the Pickard home, there is always plenty and always an invitation to "come join us." And while many have abandoned this practice these days, Oma continues to show God's love and abundance through the meals she serves.

So no matter what time of year and no matter if it is a special occasion or just an ordinary weekend, know that there will be a unique mixture of guests assembled at the home of Oma Pickard. And as Devin returns thanks before constantly changing faces, he knows that her dinner table is just as important for God's ministry as his pulpit.

Quick Dinner Rolls

If you have never made homemade dinner rolls before, this is the recipe to get you started. In only an hour, you can have mouthwatering bread that will be irresistible with any meal. You'll look like a professional baker in no time flat! (Photo on page 70.)

YIELD: 12 TO 15 SERVINGS

3 (.25-ounce) packets dry active yeast

1 3/4 cups very warm water (110 degrees to 115 degrees)

1/2 cup honey or agave nectar

1/2 cup (1 stick) butter, melted

2 teaspoons salt

2 large eggs

5 to 6 cups all-purpose flour

Lightly grease a rimmed baking sheet. Place the yeast and the water in the bowl of an electric mixer and let stand for 5 minutes. With the mixer speed on low, blend in the honey, melted butter, salt, and eggs. Gradually add the flour 1 cup at a time. Add 5 cups of flour and add an additional cup if necessary. The mixture should pull away from the side of the bowl.

With a sharp knife, cut the dough into 24 equal portions. Shape as you wish and place on the prepared baking sheet with about an inch of space between each roll. Set aside in a warm place away from drafts to rise for 20 minutes or until doubled in size.

Preheat the oven to 400 degrees. Bake for 25 minutes or until golden brown. Serve immediately.

NOTE: *If the honey in your pantry has started to crystallize, remove the lid and place it in the microwave on low power for 20 seconds. Replace the lid, let the crystals dissolve, and it's as good as new.*

was learning the recipe, she was told to dip her hand in the lard bucket, curl her fingers, and then pull them out. "That's how much you use to make biscuits!" she proudly declared.

Today, there is no doubt in David's mind that Ruth is entertaining countless brothers and sisters in Christ with amusing stories in her heavenly home. And he is equally convinced that a plate of hot biscuits is waiting to be lovingly shared. Someday the joy of breaking bread with her will happen again for David and others who had their lives enhanced through a simple Southern biscuit.

Breaker Cornbread Muffins

Farmers will tell you that when a green tomato just starts to turn a bit pink, it's called a breaker. This recipe makes good use of those tomatoes that straddle the fence between green and ripe. I always make a big batch of these muffins when I have to harvest those left on the vine before a frost.

Yield: 20 muffins

4 tablespoons butter, divided

2 cups seeded, peeled, and chopped pink tomatoes*

2 cups self-rising cornmeal

1/4 cup sugar

5 large eggs

1 (16-ounce) container sour cream

Preheat the oven to 450 degrees. Lightly grease 20 muffin cups.

Place 2 tablespoons of the butter in a large skillet over medium-high heat. When melted, add the tomatoes and sauté for 8 minutes, stirring occasionally.

In a medium bowl combine the cornmeal and sugar. In another medium bowl whisk together the eggs and sour cream until well blended. Melt the remaining 2 tablespoons butter in the microwave on low power for 30 seconds and add to the egg mixture, blending well.

Add the tomatoes and egg mixture to the cornmeal and stir until moistened. Divide the batter evenly among the muffin cups, filling 2/3 full. Bake 15 minutes or until a tester inserted in the center comes out clean. Serve warm.

NOTE: *Any leftover muffins freeze well. Package, label, and freeze, then use within 1 month for the best quality.*

---

* A firm green tomato that is just starting to blush pink.

Peppered Bacon Biscuits

My husband, George, is constantly bringing home peppered bacon, and I like to use the leftovers from breakfast to crumble into these fantastic biscuits for dinner. They always get a thumbs-up from George and everyone else at the table.

YIELD: AROUND 20 BISCUITS

....

2 1/4 cups self-rising flour

5 slices peppered bacon, cooked
   and crumbled

4 tablespoons (1/2 stick) cold
   butter, cut into pieces

1 1/4 cups buttermilk

....

In a medium bowl combine the flour and bacon. Cut in the butter with a pastry blender or 2 forks until the mixture resembles small peas. Cover and refrigerate 7 minutes.

Preheat the oven to 450 degrees. Lightly grease a rimmed baking sheet.

Add the buttermilk to the flour mixture and stir until moistened. Turn the dough out onto a heavily floured surface and knead 8 times. Roll to 1/2-inch thickness and cut with a 2-inch round cutter. Transfer the biscuits to the prepared baking sheet and bake 12 to 15 minutes or until golden brown. Serve warm.

NOTE: *Store leftovers tightly wrapped at room temperature.*

Chocolate-Chip Pumpkin Bread

This delicious quick bread gives you one loaf to serve and one to send home with your dinner guest. Spread thick slices with softened butter or top with freshly whipped cream. It is also terrific on an appetizer tray with fresh fruit.

YIELD: 2 LOAVES

3 1/3 cups all-purpose flour

3 cups sugar

4 teaspoons pumpkin pie spice

2 teaspoons baking soda

1 teaspoon salt

1/2 teaspoon baking powder

4 large eggs

1 (15-ounce) can solid-pack pumpkin

2/3 cup water

2/3 cup vegetable oil

2 cups semisweet chocolate chips

1 cup chopped, toasted pecans or walnuts

Preheat the oven to 350 degrees. Lightly grease 2 loaf pans. In a large bowl combine the flour, sugar, pumpkin pie spice, baking soda, salt, and baking powder. Make a well in the center.

In a medium bowl combine the eggs, pumpkin, water, and oil. Whisk until smooth and pour into the well of the flour mixture. Stir just until moistened and add the chocolate chips and pecans. Evenly divide the dough between the 2 prepared loaf pans and bake 1 hour and 10 minutes.

Insert a cake tester in the center and make sure it comes out clean. If not, bake 5 minutes longer. Cool in the pans on a wire rack for 10 minutes before removing and cooling completely. Use immediately or wrap in freezer paper and freeze up to 4 months.

NOTE: *You can substitute golden raisins for the chocolate chips if desired.*

Sorghum Buttermilk Loaf

It is going to be difficult to keep your family out of this bread when you make it the day before serving for dinner. The aroma of it baking in the oven is nothing short of intoxicating. You can substitute honey for the sorghum syrup if desired.

YIELD: 10 TO 12 SERVINGS

....

2 1/2 cups all-purpose flour

1 teaspoon baking powder

1 teaspoon baking soda

1 teaspoon salt

1 1/2 cups buttermilk

1/2 cup sorghum syrup

4 tablespoons butter, softened

....

Preheat the oven to 350 degrees. Grease a loaf pan.

In a medium bowl combine the flour, baking powder, baking soda, and salt. Make a well in the center and add the buttermilk, sorghum, and butter. Stir well to combine and transfer the batter to the prepared loaf pan. Bake 85 to 90 minutes or until a cake tester inserted in the center comes out clean. Remove from the pan and cool completely on a wire rack before slicing and serving.

NOTE: *This bread freezes very well. Package cut slices in a freezer bag, label, freeze, and use within 1 month.*

Sunday Dinner Memories

S ome people are instantly likeable, and Carl Terry falls into that category. *Jovial* would be a great adjective for describing him, and you feel better just for knowing him.

It's those qualities that made him a successful pastor in the Methodist church for nearly fifty years. And while he no longer preaches, his ministry is far from over. He now volunteers at several different nursing homes scattered all over Birmingham, Alabama. "I love getting people out of their rooms. It's interesting how you can get them to talk to you by changing what they see," he observes.

Carl has a backpack full of treats that he carries with him when he visits his friends. On a rather dark, stormy day last winter, Carl went to see his buddy Lewis, who is in a wheelchair and looks forward to their weekly rolls around the halls. Lewis liked routine and insisted on the same path each time. He wanted to go past the nurses' station first, then down by the library and TV room, and finally to the lunch-room before it was time to "head on back."

Carl was usually there by nine, but was running a little late on this particular day. Lewis was anxiously waiting on him, all dressed and wearing his ever-present Crimson Tide baseball cap.

They took their usual route and ended up in the lunchroom. Though it was really too early for lunch, Carl pulled a package of pea-nut butter crackers out of his backpack for the two of them to share. As they sat there munching on crackers and sipping water, a new young therapist stopped to see to them and Lewis talked up a storm. Carl pulled out another package of crackers and she joined them, saying peanut butter crackers were her favorites. Time flew by as they laughed and ate crackers.

Both Carl and Lewis hated to hear a page over the intercom telling the therapist to return to building B. She hugged them both and thanked them for what would be her lunch and for entertaining her. As she was walking away, Lewis looked at Carl and said that was the finest lunch he ever had. Then he added, "What I wouldn't give to be seventy-five again!"

Sweet Skillet Cornbread

A skillet made of cast iron can go straight from the oven to the dinner table. Make sure you have softened butter pats ready for this feast, along with a pot of pinto beans and greens.

YIELD: 8 TO 10 SERVINGS

2 1/2 cups all-purpose flour

1 cup plain cornmeal

1 cup sugar

2 1/2 tablespoons baking powder

1 tablespoon salt

1/4 teaspoon paprika

5 large eggs

2 cups whole milk

3/4 cup butter, melted

1/3 cup water

1/4 cup vegetable oil

1 cup fresh corn kernels

Preheat the oven to 400 degrees. Generously grease a 12-inch cast-iron skillet and place in the oven while it preheats.

In a medium bowl combine the flour, cornmeal, sugar, baking powder, salt, and paprika. In the bowl of an electric mixer, beat the eggs for 3 minutes on high. Reduce the mixer speed to low and add the milk, melted butter, water, and oil. Stir in the flour mixture, being careful not to overmix. Gently fold in the corn. Transfer the batter to the hot skillet.

Bake 55 minutes or until a cake tester inserted in the center comes out with moist crumbs. Cut into wedges and serve from the skillet or invert onto a serving plate and cut into wedges.

NOTE: *Leftovers freeze very well. Package, label, freeze, and use within 1 month for the best quality.*

Sweet Potato Cornbread

Now, before you start saying, "Don't go messin' with my cornbread!" give this option a chance. It is beautiful next to barbecue and looks like fall. Plus, it's a delicious way to use up any leftover mashed sweet potatoes.

YIELD: 8 SERVINGS

2 cups self-rising cornmeal

3 tablespoons sugar

5 large eggs

2 cups cooked and mashed sweet
  potatoes

1 (8-ounce) container sour
  cream

1/2 cup (1 stick) butter, melted

Grease a 10-inch cast-iron skillet and place in the oven. Preheat the oven to 425 degrees.

In a medium bowl stir together the cornmeal and sugar. In another medium bowl whisk together the eggs, sweet potatoes, sour cream, and melted butter. Add to the cornmeal mixture and stir just until moistened.

Remove the skillet from the oven and transfer the batter to the hot skillet. Bake 35 minutes or until golden brown. Invert onto a serving plate and cut into wedges. Serve warm.

NOTE: *Leftovers freeze very well. Package, label, freeze, and use within 1 month for the best quality.*

No Need to Knead Wheat Bread

Let the wonder of leavening and buttermilk do all the work for you with this bread. Toasting cut slices under the broiler or in the toaster before serving really brings out the whole wheat nutty taste.

YIELD: 10 TO 12 SERVINGS

2 1/4 cups whole wheat flour

1 cup ground pecans or walnuts

3/4 cup firmly packed light
  brown sugar

2 1/2 teaspoons baking powder

1 teaspoon baking soda

3/4 teaspoon salt

1 1/2 cups buttermilk

Preheat the oven to 350 degrees. Grease a loaf pan.

In a medium bowl combine the flour, pecans, brown sugar, baking powder, baking soda, and salt. Make a well in the center and add the buttermilk. Mix well until combined. Transfer to the prepared loaf pan and bake 1 hour or until a cake tester inserted in the center comes out clean. Remove from the pan and cool completely on a wire rack before slicing and serving.

NOTE: *When completely cool, wrap the loaf in plastic wrap, then in aluminum foil and store at room temperature.*

Milk Rolls

Baking rolls in a milk bath has been done for years and gives the rolls a tender, sweet flavor that is wonderfully moist. You can use frozen roll dough if you don't want to go to the trouble of making your own, but one bite of these will convince you that it was worth the effort.

YIELD: 6 TO 8 SERVINGS

3 cups all-purpose flour

1/4 cup very warm water (110 degrees)

1 1/2 teaspoons dry active yeast

1 tablespoon canola oil

Pinch of salt

1 (13.5-ounce) can coconut milk, divided

1/4 cup sugar

Place the flour in the bowl of an electric mixer and make a well in the center. Add the water and sprinkle the yeast over the top. Allow to stand for 5 minutes. Add the oil and salt. With the dough hook attached, mix slowly for 4 minutes. Gradually add 3/4 cup of the coconut milk and mix 4 minutes longer. Cover with a clean kitchen towel and set aside to rise for 2 hours.

Grease a 12-inch round baking pan. Divide the dough into 10 to 12 even dough balls and place on the prepared pan. Cover again and set aside to rise for another hour.

Preheat the oven to 375 degrees. Whisk the remaining coconut milk with the sugar. Slowly and gently pour over the rolls. Bake for 35 minutes or until golden brown. Serve warm.

NOTE: *These rolls cook beautifully in cast iron.*

SUNDAY DINNER MEMORIES

In the early 1980s, Richard Herring was living in Memphis, Tennessee, and was an interim pastor for not one but two Methodist congregations along Poplar Avenue. Since both were small, he had little trouble balancing his time between them.

Mamie Jamison was a member of the congregation who was in her eighties and lived next door to one of the churches. Mamie should have been a detective. She knew every car in the neighborhood and kept a mental record of the comings and goings of anyone who pulled into the church parking lot. It seemed to be her mission in life, and if a vehicle pulled in that was unfamiliar, she was on the phone calling the church office to see who that was.

While this type of pastime could be viewed as amusing, it quickly became a bit of a nuisance to Richard. Every Thursday he spent a day in the church office, and she never seemed to recognize his 1976 Ford Granada. He could count on the phone ringing before he even got in the door. Richard decided that she just needed to meet him in person.

So the next week when she called on the phone, Richard was ready. He asked Mamie if it would be okay for him to come over and meet her since he would be a regular until the new preacher was assigned. She agreed, but only if he came at lunchtime and brought over some hamburgers. She gave strict instructions that it shouldn't be a cheeseburger and it shouldn't have onions on it because that would mess up her digestive system. Richard was tickled, and it soon became a weekly standing lunch date between the two of them. They would have lunch promptly at noon, and he knew he needed to walk out her door by twelve forty-five because her "stories" came on the TV at one.

After six months, Richard was reassigned and a new preacher was in place. Before he left, Richard placed a note in the desk for the new preacher, outlining the hamburger toppings and time requirements for getting along with the "detective" next door!

Applewood Bacon Spoon Bread

Supposedly, spoon bread was invented when a cook added too much liquid to the cornbread batter, and after baking, it literally had to be spooned out of the dish to serve. We are the lucky recipients of that "mistake," and you'll love this version enhanced by crumbled applewood smoked bacon.

YIELD: 6 TO 8 SERVINGS

1 3/4 cups milk

2/3 cup self-rising cornmeal

1/2 teaspoon salt

3/4 cup grated sharp Cheddar cheese

3 large eggs, separated

1 garlic clove, peeled and minced

1 tablespoon butter

1/4 teaspoon black pepper

1/2 cup whole kernel corn

3 slices applewood bacon, cooked and crumbled

Preheat the oven to 350 degrees. Grease a 6-cup soufflé dish. Place the milk in a heavy saucepan over medium heat. After 3 minutes, gradually add the cornmeal and salt. Bring to a slow boil, stirring constantly. Cook for 7 to 9 minutes or until thick and smooth. Remove from the heat and stir in the Cheddar, egg yolks, garlic, butter, and pepper.

In the bowl of an electric mixer, beat the egg whites at medium-high speed until soft peaks form, about 2 minutes. Stir one-fourth of the egg whites into the cornmeal mixture. Gently fold in the remaining egg whites. Fold in the corn and bacon. Transfer to the prepared dish. Bake 45 to 50 minutes or until puffed and light golden brown. Serve immediately.

NOTE: *If you can find it, cherry smoked bacon makes a great substitute for the applewood variety.*

Almost Cracklin' Cornbread

Cracklings are fried bits of pork skin that some call pork rinds. Here, bacon is a more readily available substitute. And with the addition of flour, you have a very light, airy texture.

YIELD: 8 SERVINGS

I cup plain cornmeal

I cup all-purpose flour

1/4 cup sugar

2 1/2 teaspoons baking powder

1/4 teaspoon salt

I large egg

I cup buttermilk

6 tablespoons butter, melted

9 bacon slices, cooked and
   crumbled

Preheat the oven to 400 degrees. Grease a 9-inch cast-iron skillet and place in the oven while it preheats.

In a medium bowl stir together the cornmeal, flour, sugar, baking powder, and salt. Make a well in the center. In another medium bowl combine the egg, buttermilk, melted butter, and bacon. Add to the cornmeal mixture and stir gently to combine.

Remove the skillet from the oven and transfer the batter to the hot skillet. Bake on the center rack of the oven for 25 minutes or until lightly browned. Invert onto a serving plate and cut into slices. Serve warm.

NOTE: *Peppered bacon gives this cornbread an extra punch.*

Sides

Purple Hull Pea Cakes with Summer Tomatoes

These zesty vegetable cakes get zing from Cajun seasoning. You'll notice the impact too, so don't leave it out. The hint of spice is what sets these apart from others. I love serving these with a simple salad of mixed greens.

YIELD: 6 SERVINGS

2 cups cooked purple hull peas

2 garlic cloves, peeled and minced

1 (6-ounce) package buttermilk cornbread mix

1 large egg, lightly beaten

1/4 cup sour cream

1 1/2 teaspoons Cajun or Creole seasoning

1/2 teaspoon onion salt

1 lime, cut into wedges

1 large beefsteak tomato, sliced

In a medium bowl coarsely mash the peas with a fork. Stir in the garlic, cornbread mix, egg, sour cream, seasoning, and onion salt. Grease a large griddle. When hot, drop about 1/3 cup of the batter onto the griddle and cook 2 minutes or until the edges look dry and cooked. Turn and cook 2 minutes longer. Transfer to a serving platter and continue with the remaining batter. Drizzle with lime juice and serve immediately with the tomato slices.

NOTE: *Leftovers can be reheated in a preheated 350-degree oven for 5 minutes.*

Sweet Potato Gratin

This recipe is pure magic, and I got it from my friend Helen. I love the simplicity of it, yet the depth of flavor you get from steeping the cream with herbs and spices adds a complexity that will make this dish a star. Serve it with turkey, pork, or ham.

Yield: 4 to 5 servings

---

1 cup heavy cream

3 fresh sage leaves

1 large bay leaf

1 (2-inch) piece fresh ginger, peeled and thinly sliced

1/2 teaspoon kosher salt

Pinch of cayenne pepper

1 pound sweet potatoes, peeled and thinly sliced

Place the cream in a small saucepan over medium-high heat. Add the sage, bay leaf, ginger, salt, and cayenne. Bring to a simmer and cook 1 minute. Remove from the heat, cover, and steep for 10 minutes.

Preheat the oven to 375 degrees. Grease a deep square or 9-inch round baking dish. With a slotted spoon, remove the sage, bay leaf, and ginger from the cream mixture. Discard the bay leaf and ginger. Reserve the sage leaves.

Pour 1/3 cup cream into the bottom of the baking dish. Top with half of the sweet potato slices, overlapping each slice by nearly half.

Add another 1/3 cup cream to the top and repeat with the remaining sweet potato slices and remaining 1/3 cup cream. Arrange the sage leaves on top and cover with aluminum foil. Bake 30 minutes and remove the foil. With the slotted spoon, gently mash the sweet potato slices into the cream mixture. Bake uncovered for 15 to 17 minutes longer or until the potatoes are tender. Serve warm.

NOTE: *Let the dish rest for 10 minutes before serving for the best results.*

Sunday Dinner Memories

For nearly forty-eight years, James Stevens was a fill-in minister, content to move throughout the South and take care of Baptist congregations that were in between hiring permanent clergy. He didn't stay in one place for very long, and he loved discovering new areas and meeting new people.

At one point in his traveling career back in 1968, he landed in Montgomery, Alabama, for a two-month job. It was a growing church with lots of energy and activity. James quickly found himself on a regular circuit of enjoying some of the finest food he had ever tasted.

After a few weeks, James was asked to dine after church with Sadie Webster, an elegant older lady who was always on the arm of her grandson Charles. James noticed that Sadie had impeccable taste and a beaming smile. "She laughed with her eyes," he remembers, "and I can still see it now!"

James arrived on Ms. Sadie's front porch at the appointed time of one o'clock and was greeted with a tall glass of fruit tea. He was told to go ahead and take a seat at the table while she fixed their plates.

As James took his place, he noticed a huge spot on the otherwise perfectly ironed tablecloth. Not wanting Ms. Sadie to be embarrassed, he moved the floral arrangement over so that the stain was partially covered. She returned with plates of roasted chicken, potatoes, carrots, and hoecakes. And to his surprise, without a word she moved the floral arrangement back to the original place, completely revealing the tablecloth stain.

James thoroughly enjoyed the delicious meal and lively conversation with Ms. Sadie. He appreciated her ease in talking to him about a wide range of topics and realized the time flew by quickly; they sat at the table for over two hours. He was thinking it was probably time to leave when Sadie asked if he had noticed the stain on the tablecloth. Trying to act like it was no big deal, he said that he had, and to his surprise, Sadie said she was glad.

"My husband spilled wine on that spot when our son announced they were expecting Charles," she stated. "It reminds me of a marvelous day when we were so richly blessed, and I love seeing the stain," she continued.

At that moment, James realized he had just been blessed as well. Not by a meal, but by a memory that was kept alive in her home by a well-loved spot that was no longer a dreaded stain, but a beautiful reminder of a blessing from God.

Grilled Stuffed Hot Peppers

Have these peppers stuffed ahead of time and then add to the grill with the meat you are serving. No matter how many I serve, I never seem to have made enough.

YIELD: 10 SERVINGS

1 (8-ounce) package cream cheese, softened

1/4 cup shredded sharp Cheddar cheese

2 bacon slices, cooked and crumbled

1 green onion, chopped

1 teaspoon lime juice

1/4 teaspoon garlic salt

14 large jalapeño peppers, halved lengthwise and seeded

2 tablespoons chopped fresh cilantro

Preheat the grill to medium-high heat. In the bowl of an electric mixer, combine the cream cheese, Cheddar, bacon, green onions, lime juice, and garlic salt. Mix on low speed until well combined, about 1 minute. Spoon the mixture into the jalapeño halves and place on a lightly greased grill rack. Place the rack on the grill and cover. Grill 8 minutes or until the bottoms of the peppers are charred. Top with the cilantro and serve warm.

NOTE : *If you aren't a heat lover, use the same mixture to stuff poblano peppers and increase the grill time to 11 minutes.*

Mushrooms Au Gratin

Move on over, potatoes! Mushrooms take the spotlight here in a dish that is ready to serve in a flash. Just for fun, top it with seasoned bread crumbs in addition to or instead of the cheese.

YIELD: 4 TO 6 SERVINGS

....

2 tablespoons butter

1 (16-ounce) package sliced
  mushrooms

1/3 cup sour cream

1 tablespoon all-purpose flour

1/4 teaspoon onion salt

1/8 teaspoon black pepper

1/4 cup chopped fresh parsley

1/2 cup shredded Swiss or
  Gruyere cheese

....

Preheat the oven to 425 degrees. Place the butter in a large ovenproof skillet over medium-high heat. When melted, add the mushrooms, sour cream, flour, onion salt, and pepper. Cook 5 minutes and remove from the heat. Sprinkle evenly with the parsley and cheese. Bake 10 minutes or until the cheese has melted and is lightly browned. Serve warm.

NOTE: *Let this dish rest for at least 5 minutes before serving for best results.*

Bacon and Blue Cheese Grits

I have managed to get even those who think they don't like blue cheese to become fans of this dish. But if you are not so sure, substitute crumbled feta or a mixture of the two. The salty bacon is a nice balance with the zippy cheese.

YIELD: 8 SERVINGS

2 cups milk

2 cups low-sodium vegetable or
chicken stock

1 cup regular grits

1 teaspoon garlic salt

1/4 cup heavy cream or half-and-half

2 large eggs, lightly beaten

2/3 cup crumbled blue cheese

6 slices bacon, cooked and crumbled

Chopped fresh parsley for garnish

Preheat the oven to 350 degrees. Lightly grease 8 (^{1}/2-cup) ramekins and place them on a baking sheet.

In a large saucepan over medium-high heat, combine the milk and stock. Bring to a boil. Whisk in the grits and garlic salt and reduce the heat to low. Cook, stirring frequently, for 10 minutes. Add the cream and continue to cook and stir for 7 minutes or until thick and smooth. Remove the pan from the heat and add the eggs and blue cheese, stirring until the cheese is completely melted. Stir in the bacon.

Divide the grits evenly among the prepared ramekins. Bake 30 minutes or until set. Garnish each with a sprinkling of fresh parsley before serving warm.

Sunday Dinner Memories

Jeremy McFarlin has been preaching most of his life, beginning at the tender age of twelve. Today he is the minister of Wildwood Valley Church of Christ in Tennessee.

He has a fun-loving spirit and likes all kinds of foods. He really does. He will eat and enjoy almost anything his congregation prepares for him, except for one item . . . green beans. Over the years he has been coaxed into trying them prepared in all kinds of ways, but the verdict always remains the same. He simply doesn't like them in any form, on any day, in any amount. So if his parishioners make the delicious Presto Pesto Green Beans (on page 130), they just have to remember there will be more for them and none for him!

When Jeremy started his ministry at Wildwood Valley, he got to know a gentleman named Max Davis. Max had the job of turning off the lights and locking the church doors, so they often saw each other at the end of the day. They got to know each other very well and appreciated each other's sense of humor.

After Jeremy had been at the church for about a year, Max moved on to his heavenly home after a valiant battle with stomach cancer. Jeremy had spent many hours sitting by Max's hospital bedside, and he still describes Max as the nicest man he has ever known.

The morning after Max died, Jeremy went to visit the Davis family. He arrived just as Mrs. Davis was feeding the children breakfast and she invited Jeremy to join them for a bacon biscuit. A few minutes later Mrs. Davis realized she had not given Jeremy anything to drink and quickly scampered around the kitchen to make it right.

Even now, Jeremy remembers that lovely, simple breakfast meal fondly because it underlined how remarkable the Davis family is. Somehow in their moment of incredible loss and pain, they were willing to serve him rather than just focusing on themselves. The powerful lesson of being a giver at all times was emphasized that morning, and when Jeremy later preached the funeral, tears flowed without ceasing. As Jeremy cried through the comfort he was attempting to bestow on others that bleak winter day, he knew that Max Davis went from being a gift to all who knew him here to a wonderful gift in heaven.

You Be Sweet Roasted Carrots

I love carrots prepared any way and am just as happy munching on them raw as when they are softly baked. This recipe from my friend Rhonda has a bit of salt, a little sweetness, and some zing from citrus zest. It is especially beautiful when you use a mixture of orange, purple, white, yellow, and red carrots. I serve this side dish with roasted chicken or turkey.

YIELD: 4 SERVINGS

2 pounds carrots, peeled and cut in 2-inch pieces

1 1/2 teaspoons salt, divided

2 tablespoons olive oil

2 tablespoons honey or sorghum syrup

1/4 teaspoon black pepper

1 tablespoon finely grated orange zest

Place the carrots in a large saucepan full of water and add 1/2 teaspoon of the salt. Bring to a boil over medium-high heat and cook 4 minutes.

Preheat the oven to 400 degrees. Lightly grease a rimmed baking sheet. In a small bowl whisk together the olive oil, honey, pepper, and the remaining 1 teaspoon salt.

Drain the carrots well and place in a single layer on the prepared baking sheet. Drizzle evenly with the honey mixture. Bake 35 to 40 minutes, shaking the pan every 10 minutes. Transfer to a serving bowl and toss with the orange zest. Serve warm.

NOTE: *If you purchase carrots with the tops attached, remove them as soon as you get home. The tops pull moisture from the roots and hasten decay.*

Grits and Greens

This grits recipe has quickly become one of my favorites because it includes everything I love in one dish. The combination of sausage, cheese, greens, and hot sauce could not be better when folded into creamy grits. Have extra hot sauce available for the heat lovers around your table.

Yield: 8 servings

1 cup low-sodium chicken stock

1/3 cup half-and-half

1/2 teaspoon salt, divided

1 cup water

1/2 cup regular grits

1 tablespoon olive oil

3 ounces dry chorizo or summer sausage, chopped

8 large fresh collard green leaves, chopped

2 teaspoons cider vinegar

1/2 teaspoon sugar

1/2 cup shredded sharp Cheddar cheese

1/4 cup grated Parmesan cheese

1 tablespoon butter

1/2 teaspoon hot sauce

1/4 teaspoon black pepper

In a medium saucepan over high heat, combine the stock, half-and-half, and 1/4 teaspoon of the salt. Add the water and bring to a boil. Gradually whisk in the grits, cover, reduce the heat to medium-low, and simmer. Stir occasionally and cook 15 minutes or until thickened.

Heat the olive oil in a large skillet over medium-high heat. Add the chorizo and cook 2 minutes. Add the collards, cider vinegar, sugar, and the remaining 1/4 teaspoon salt. Cook, stirring constantly, for 2 minutes.

Whisk the Cheddar, Parmesan, butter, hot sauce, and pepper into the grits. Transfer to a serving bowl. Top with the collard green mixture and serve hot.

NOTE: *You can increase the heat by substituting pepper jack for the Cheddar cheese in this recipe.*

SUNDAY DINNER MEMORIES

Discipline is a cherished commodity when dealing when children, and Joseph Green especially appreciated it as a youth minister with the Presbyterian church in Columbia, South Carolina.

This was Joseph's first job, and he took the responsibility very seriously. He appreciated the enthusiasm of the youngsters in his congregation, but realized he needed to harness that in a healthy way. It was his biggest job challenge.

Since Joseph was young and single, he was frequently asked to Sunday dinner after church, and being on a tight budget, he hungrily accepted. After he had been at the church about four months, he accepted an invitation to dine at the home of Edna and Frank Fisher. Their three children were a part of Joseph's youth group and were some of the best-behaved children he had ever seen. He was anxious to see if they were as well disciplined at home as they were during church activities.

When Joseph arrived at their house, the kids were in the backyard, and he welcomed the opportunity to spend time with Edna and Frank. The two of them worked in perfect harmony in the kitchen. Joseph had never been to their home before and noticed it was tidy and tastefully decorated. He also noticed three miniature doghouses on a shelf there in the kitchen. Beside each was a different toy dog. He was just about to inquire about the meaning when Edna said it was time to eat, and a large pan of red beans and rice caught his attention.

The kids came scrambling into the kitchen and soon settled into their seats at a bench-style table. Joseph was passed smoked sausage, squares of cornbread, and that incredible-looking pan of red beans and rice. As the dishes made their way around the table, two of the kids got into a tiff about the end pieces of cornbread. One got the last corner piece, and according to his sister, he knew she wanted it and grabbed it anyway!

Edna didn't say a word but got up and moved two of the toy dogs into the doghouses. Immediately the verbal sparring stopped, and the meal proceeded without incident.

Joseph helped clean up after the meal was over and was thrilled when Edna insisted on him taking the leftovers for his dinner the following day. But he couldn't leave without asking about the toy dogs, which he noticed at some point had been moved out of the houses.

Frank explained that whenever a child exhibited unbecoming actions, their dog was moved into the doghouse. Remarkably, it was seldom necessary to say a word. That silent rebuke eliminated the need for any further discussion on the matter. It was brilliant, and Joseph said a grateful prayer of thanks for the cornbread that showed him the impact of a gentle reminder.

Peanut Fried Cauliflower

Sometimes seeing the word **fried** *in a recipe title can make you skip right over it because the perception is it takes too much time to prepare. This one is quickly done in a cast-iron skillet, and it's simply sprinkled with a drizzle of vinegar to serve. You will obsess over the nutty overtones it gets from the oil and crushed peanuts.*

YIELD: 6 TO 8 SERVINGS

I cauliflower head, broken into
   bite-size florets
2 cups peanut or sunflower oil
1/4 cup all-purpose flour
I tablespoon ground peanuts

2 teaspoons paprika
I teaspoon salt
1/2 teaspoon black pepper
2 tablespoons malt or cider
   vinegar

Bring a large saucepan of water to a boil over high heat. Drop in the cauliflower florets and boil for 2 minutes. Put the oil in a deep skillet and place over medium-high heat. Place the flour, peanuts, paprika, salt, and pepper in a large zip-top bag.

Drain the cauliflower and immediately drop it into the zip-top bag. Shake to evenly coat and transfer to the hot oil. Working in batches if necessary, fry the cauliflower for 2 minutes or until light golden brown. Drain on paper towels and serve hot with a drizzle of the vinegar.

NOTE: *This is equally delicious when served with your favorite cheese dip.*

Crunchy Yellow Carrot and Squash Casserole

Yellow carrots are a new option in the produce bin, along with purple and red varieties. They provide a nice backdrop with yellow squash in this recipe. Of course, you can always use the orange version as a substitute.

YIELD: 6 SERVINGS

....

1 pound yellow carrots, peeled and sliced

1 pound yellow squash, sliced

4 slices bacon, cooked and crumbled

2 shallots, peeled and chopped

1 1/4 cups round buttery cracker crumbs, divided

1 large egg, beaten

1/2 cup milk or half-and-half

1 (2-ounce) jar diced pimientos, drained

1/2 teaspoon onion or garlic salt

1/4 teaspoon black pepper

....

Place the carrots and squash in a steamer basket over boiling water. Cover and steam 10 minutes. Drain well, mashing any excess moisture out with a wooden spoon. Place in a medium bowl.

In a large skillet over medium heat, cook the bacon until crisp. Drain on paper towels and crumble when cool enough to handle.

Preheat the oven to 350 degrees and lightly grease a 11 x 7-inch baking dish.

With the skillet still over medium heat, add the shallots and sauté 4 minutes. Put in the bowl with the carrots and squash and add 3/4 cup of the cracker crumbs. Stir in the egg, milk, pimientos, onion salt, and pepper. Transfer to the prepared baking dish and sprinkle with the remaining 1/2 cup cracker crumbs. Bake uncovered for 45 minutes or until light golden brown. Allow to stand 5 minutes before serving warm.

NOTE: *Leftovers freeze very well. Package, label, freeze, and use within 1 month for the best quality.*

Layered Ham and Potato Cheese Casserole

This dish is so lovely served next to a simple salad of mixed greens and hot, steamy bread. You can substitute cooked turkey, pork, or chicken for the ham if you wish.

Yield: 6 servings

---

4 tablespoons butter

1/3 cup chopped sweet onions

2 tablespoons all-purpose flour

2 cups whole milk or half-and-half

1 1/2 cups shredded sharp Cheddar cheese

4 1/4 cups thinly sliced potatoes

3 cups chopped cooked ham

1 1/2 cups coarse plain bread crumbs or panko

Preheat the oven to 350 degrees. Lightly grease a 2-quart deep baking dish.

Place the butter in a large skillet over medium heat. When melted, add the onions and sauté until soft, about 4 minutes. Blend in the flour and gradually stir in the milk. Cook 5 minutes, stirring constantly until thick. Add the Cheddar and stir until completely melted.

Layer one-third of the potatoes, one-third of the ham, and one-third of the cheese sauce in that order in the prepared baking dish. Repeat the layers, ending with the sauce. Bake 25 minutes, then top with the bread crumbs. Cook 25 to 30 minutes longer or until the potatoes are tender and the top is golden brown. Let rest 5 minutes before serving warm.

NOTE: *I like using a soufflé dish for making this recipe. Also, a mandolin is a handy tool for thinly slicing vegetables such as the potatoes in this dish.*

Summer Squash and Cornbread Casserole

The best of both the vegetable harvest and the cast-iron skillet are combined in this go-with-anything casserole. It can be made ahead if you are in a time crunch.

Yield: 6 servings

2 tablespoons butter

1 tablespoon vegetable oil

1 sweet onion, peeled and chopped

1 garlic clove, peeled and minced

2 tablespoons chopped red bell peppers

2 cups thinly sliced zucchini

2 cups thinly sliced yellow squash

3 cups crumbled cornbread

2 cups shredded sharp Cheddar cheese, divided

2 large eggs

2/3 cup heavy cream or half-and-half

1 tablespoon chopped fresh parsley

1 teaspoon chopped fresh thyme

1 teaspoon black pepper

1/2 teaspoon paprika

1/4 teaspoon cayenne pepper

Place the butter and oil in a large skillet over medium heat. When hot, add the onions, garlic, and red peppers. Cook, stirring occasionally, for 5 minutes.

Preheat the oven to 350 degrees. Lightly grease a 9 x 13-inch baking dish.

Add the zucchini and squash to the skillet and cook 10 minutes longer. Place the cornbread, 1 1/2 cups of the Cheddar, eggs, cream, parsley, thyme, black pepper, paprika, and cayenne in a large bowl. Stir to combine. Add the squash mixture and blend well. Transfer to the prepared baking dish. Top with the remaining 1/2 cup Cheddar. Bake 35 minutes or until hot and bubbly. Serve warm.

NOTE: *This recipe benefits from resting for at least 5 minutes after removing from the oven.*

Green Olive Potato Salad

The distinctive flavor in this salad comes from using Greek yogurt. It also lightens up the calorie count, making it acceptable to be on everyone's dinner plate. Olives take the place of ordinary pickle relish.

YIELD: 8 TO 10 SERVINGS

2 pounds red potatoes, cut in
  3/4-inch cubes

3/4 teaspoon garlic salt, divided

1 (6-ounce) container plain
  Greek yogurt

1/2 cup mayonnaise

1 tablespoon chopped fresh
  parsley

1 tablespoon Dijon mustard

1/4 teaspoon black pepper

1/4 cup chopped celery

1 large shallot, peeled and
  chopped

3 tablespoons chopped
  pimiento- or garlic-stuffed
  green olives

2 hard-boiled large eggs, peeled
  and chopped

Fresh snipped chives for garnish

Place the potatoes and 1/4 teaspoon of the garlic salt in a large saucepan and add enough water to cover. Place over high heat and bring to a boil, then reduce the heat to low, cover, and simmer 12 to 15 minutes or until the potatoes are just tender. Drain and set aside to cool for 20 minutes.

In a large bowl whisk together the yogurt, mayonnaise, parsley, Dijon, pepper, and the remaining 1/2 teaspoon garlic salt. Gently stir in the celery, shallots, olives, and eggs. Fold in the cooled potatoes. Cover and refrigerate at least 45 minutes or up to one day. Garnish with snipped chives before serving.

NOTE: *Do not substitute Russet potatoes for the red potatoes. They will fall apart after cooking.*

SUNDAY DINNER MEMORIES

Although known more for horses and bluegrass, there are plenty of rolling hills in Kentucky. That's what Henry Lyles counts as the most beautiful part of his home state. And because he spent his career moving around with the Methodist church, he has seen his fair share.

Back in the 1970s, he was in Frankfort and got to know Doug and Mary Ann Miller. Both were very active in the church along with their six children. Even though they saw each other frequently at church, Henry had been there several years before he was asked to join them for Sunday dinner. He happily accepted.

It was a rather cold, gray fall day, and Henry was grateful for the opportunity to warm his chilled bones at their cheerful home. He was greeted with the aroma of roasting beef and handed a cup of warm cider as soon as he entered. It was just what he wanted, and he knew from that moment on he was in for a treat.

With all of the kids pitching in, it wasn't long before the long kitchen table was brimming with platters and bowls of delicious-looking food. Henry was especially drawn to the turnip greens that were steaming hot near his place at the table. They smelled just like those his grandmother used to make, and he could hardly wait to dig in.

Expecting to be called on for giving the blessing, he was ready.

But Doug called on their daughter Karen, who was around nine years old. Instead of a typical prayer of returning thanks, Karen sang her blessing, and Henry was totally charmed. As she finished, the entire family sang the chorus of "I Need Thee Every Hour" before Doug said amen and the meal began.

He later discovered from Doug and Mary Ann that the practice was started years earlier, with each child singing their prayer. It was a way of bringing the family closer, and even now, it continues to be a tradition not just in the Miller family but in the Lyles family as well.

Lemon Pesto Potatoes

I love the citrus zing given to ordinary potatoes in this recipe. And don't let the fact that your herb garden might not be as abundant as usual keep you from using pesto in recipes. The store-bought versions are good for those in-a-pinch moments when you may not have time to make your own.

YIELD: 4 SERVINGS

12 small red potatoes, unpeeled and diced

1 large lemon, zested and juiced

1 (4-ounce) jar prepared pesto sauce

2 tablespoons chopped toasted pecans

Preheat the grill to medium. Spray a large piece of heavy-duty aluminum foil on one side with cooking spray. Place the potatoes in the center of the foil and sprinkle with the lemon zest and juice. Create a foil packet, rolling up the sides to seal. Place on the grill away from direct heat for 25 minutes.

Remove and carefully open the foil packet. Transfer to a serving bowl and add the pesto, tossing to lightly coat. Garnish with the pecans and serve warm.

NOTE: *If using homemade pesto, measure 1/2 cup.*

Fresh Corn Polenta with Cherry Tomatoes

I am a huge fan of anything that has a cornmeal or polenta base. I like this side dish with grilled fish or poultry. Add another side dish of slow-cooked green beans and you're ready to eat!

YIELD: 4 SERVINGS

3 cups low-sodium chicken stock

1 cup polenta or coarsely ground grits

1 cup fresh whole kernel corn

2 tablespoons butter

1 teaspoon seasoned or celery salt

12 cherry tomatoes, quartered

1 tablespoon extra-virgin olive oil

1/4 teaspoon garlic salt

1/8 teaspoon black pepper

Shaved Parmesan cheese for garnish

Place the stock in a medium saucepan over high heat and bring to a boil. Add the polenta, corn, butter, and seasoned salt. Reduce the heat to low and simmer uncovered for 7 minutes, stirring occasionally.

Place the tomatoes in a small bowl and drizzle with the olive oil, then sprinkle with the garlic salt and pepper.

Serve the polenta in shallow bowls and top with the tomatoes. Garnish with the Parmesan and serve warm.

NOTE: *The tomatoes can be made up to 1 day ahead of time. Bring to room temperature before serving.*

Garlic and Green Smashed Potatoes

I would guess that mashed potatoes rank near the top of comfort food lists. I love to add little extras in the creamy goodness, and this recipe uses garlic and herbs to ramp up the flavor.

YIELD: 10 SERVINGS

3 pounds Yukon gold potatoes, peeled and diced

2 tablespoons onion salt

2 cups half-and-half

6 garlic cloves, peeled and minced

1/4 cup grated Parmesan cheese

3 tablespoons chopped fresh parsley

3 tablespoons chopped fresh chives

2 tablespoons butter, softened, cut in pieces

1/2 teaspoon black pepper

1/4 teaspoon cayenne pepper

1/8 teaspoon paprika

In a large saucepan cover the potatoes with water and place over medium-high heat. Add the onion salt and bring to a boil. Reduce the heat to medium and cook until the potatoes are tender, around 15 minutes. Drain and gently crush with a potato masher. Add the half-and-half, garlic, Parmesan, parsley, chives, butter, black pepper, cayenne, and paprika. Stir to combine and serve warm.

NOTE: *Leftovers freeze well. Package, label, and freeze, then use within 2 months for the best quality.*

Presto Pesto Green Beans

This recipe is ready to serve quickly with minimal effort. You can adjust the cooking time to get the beans a bit softer if you desire, but I like the distinct crunch they retain with only five minutes of cooking. And just for fun: This recipe is dedicated to Jeremy McFarlin (page 110)!

Yield: 8 servings

1 teaspoon salt, divided
1 cup packed fresh basil
1 large garlic clove, peeled
2 tablespoons pine nuts
1/4 cup extra-virgin olive oil

1/3 cup coarsely grated Parmesan cheese
1/4 teaspoon black pepper
2 pounds fresh green beans, trimmed

Place a large Dutch oven of water over high heat and add 1/2 teaspoon of the salt. Cover and bring to a boil.

Place the basil, garlic, pine nuts, and the remaining 1/2 teaspoon salt in the bowl of a food processor. Pulse until finely chopped. With the processor running, slowly add the olive oil down the shoot. Scrape down the sides and stir in the Parmesan and pepper. Add more salt if desired and transfer to a large bowl.

Add the beans to the boiling water and cook uncovered for 5 minutes. Drain and add immediately to the pesto bowl. Stir to evenly coat. Serve immediately.

NOTE: *The pesto can be made up to a day ahead if necessary. Bring to room temperature before using.*

Milk Baked Corn

Sweet corn is kicked up a bit with spices as it cooks in a yummy milk bath. I like this served with poultry or any lemony grilled fish fillets.

YIELD: 6 SERVINGS

3 tablespoons butter

I small red bell pepper, seeded and chopped

I large shallot, peeled and chopped

3 tablespoons all-purpose flour

I teaspoon garlic salt

1/4 teaspoon paprika

1/4 teaspoon dry mustard

1/4 teaspoon cayenne pepper

1/4 teaspoon black pepper

I large egg yolk

I cup milk or half-and-half

2 cups fresh whole kernel corn

2/3 cup dry plain bread crumbs

Preheat the oven to 400 degrees. Lightly grease a 1 1/2-quart baking dish.

Melt the butter in a large skillet over medium heat. Add the red peppers and shallots and cook 5 to 7 minutes. In a small bowl combine the flour, garlic salt, paprika, dry mustard, cayenne, and pepper. In another small bowl lightly beat the egg yolk.

When the red peppers and shallots are softened, stir in the flour mixture and cook 1 minute longer. Gradually add the milk and bring to a boil, stirring constantly.

Slowly stir 1/4 cup of the hot milk mixture into the egg yolk to temper it. Add the egg mixture and the corn into the skillet, stirring to combine. Transfer to the prepared baking dish and top evenly with the bread crumbs.

Bake 25 to 28 minutes or until golden brown and bubbly. Let stand 5 minutes before serving warm.

NOTE: *Leftovers freeze very well. Package, label, freeze, and use within 2 months for the best quality.*

SUNDAY DINNER MEMORIES

Tony Rushing knew that he wanted to marry Rebecca the moment he laid eyes on her. He had never seen a more beautiful girl in his life, and a year later, they were married.

After a honeymoon in Chicago, they settled into their new home in Orlando, Florida, where Tony was employed as a youth minister in the Baptist church. It was 1977, and one of their wedding gifts was a new appliance called a microwave oven. Rebecca could hardly wait to try it out and made a big deal of how she was going to use it to make the first dinner in their new house that evening.

Tony went into work and thought all day long about the first cooked meal Rebecca would ever make for him. He tried to imagine what it would be . . . maybe his favorite chicken dish, or some of the corn-on-the-cob he had spied in the refrigerator. He knew it would be delicious because Rebecca's mom was an excellent cook and surely those same skills had been passed on to her.

As he drove home late that afternoon, he prepared himself mentally, saying that no matter what she had on the table, he was going to like it and brag on it. When he got home, he was pleased to see the dining room table set with the dishes they had picked out together for their registry.

Rebecca had gone to a lot of trouble to make everything look beautiful, and the effort was not lost on Tony. She sent him to change into more comfortable clothes while she put the finishing touches on the meal. He all but dashed back to the table to see candles lit and the lights dimmed.

Freshly buttered ears of corn were brought in first and smelled scrumptious. Then came brown-and-serve rolls that he oohed and aahed over. Finally, Rebecca announced that she was bringing the main dish, which was chicken casserole. But just as she was entering the dining room, she tripped on the threshold and the chicken casserole went flying all over the floor.

After making sure Rebecca was all right, Tony had the jobs of mopping up the casserole and drying many tears. They ended up having a romantic dinner of corn and rolls. Every year until Rebecca's passing in 2013, they enjoyed the same menu on their anniversary. It remains his favorite meal of all time.

Fresh Asparagus and Cream

If there was ever a good time for serving fresh asparagus, it's in the spring when you want to really to impress your guests. Although the recipe calls for fresh chives, feel free to substitute chopped parsley or thyme from your emerging perennial herb garden.

YIELD: 6 SERVINGS

1 1/4 teaspoons salt, divided

2 pounds fresh asparagus, trimmed

2 tablespoons lemon juice

1 teaspoon lemon zest

1/8 teaspoon black pepper

1/2 cup sour cream or crème fraiche

2 tablespoons half-and-half

1 tablespoon freshly snipped chives for garnish

Place a large saucepan of water over high heat and bring to a boil. Add 1 teaspoon of the salt and the asparagus. Cook 4 minutes. Place ice and water in a large bowl. When the asparagus is done, use tongs to transfer to the ice water and let soak for 4 minutes. In a medium bowl whisk together the remaining 1/4 teaspoon salt, lemon juice, lemon zest, pepper, sour cream, and half-and-half until smooth. Drain the asparagus on paper towels and transfer to a serving platter. Spoon the sauce across the asparagus and garnish with the chives. Serve immediately.

NOTE: *Try to select asparagus spears that are as close to the same diameter as possible for even cooking.*

Vegetable Mac and Cheese

Adding a mixture of vegetables to a family favorite is a great way to have the best of both worlds. Use any mixture of frozen vegetables you happen to have on hand. I like those with a combination of peppers, broccoli, and carrots.

Yield: 6 servings

8 ounces rotini pasta

4 tablespoons butter, divided

1 cup milk or half-and-half

4 cups frozen mixed vegetables, thawed

2 1/4 cups shredded sharp Cheddar cheese

1/4 teaspoon garlic salt

1/4 teaspoon black pepper

1/8 teaspoon cayenne pepper

1/4 cup dry seasoned bread crumbs

1 tablespoon finely grated Parmesan cheese

Cook the pasta in a large pot of boiling water according to the package directions. Preheat the oven to 400 degrees. Lightly grease an 8-inch baking dish.

In a large bowl combine 3 tablespoons of the butter with the milk, mixed vegetables, Cheddar, garlic salt, black pepper, and cayenne. Drain the pasta and add to the bowl. Stir gently to combine and transfer to the prepared baking dish.

Place the remaining 1 tablespoon butter in a small glass dish and microwave on low power for 20 seconds until melted. Add the bread crumbs and Parmesan and stir until combined. Sprinkle evenly on top of the pasta mixture. Bake 28 to 30 minutes and serve warm.

NOTE: *This dish benefits from resting at least 5 minutes after baking before it is served.*

Sunday Dinner Memories

As a general rule, men aren't famous for being huge conversationalists about their feelings. Switch that channel to sports, weather, fishing, or cars, and it's a different story altogether. Andrew Jenkins describes himself no differently, and even now, at eighty years old, he admits he is still learning how to communicate.

Andrew grew up in a family filled with boys. He had three brothers and more male cousins than he could count. They lived within a stone's throw of one another, and the houses seemed to belong to all of them. "No matter where we were," he says, "we had a relative close by, which was great if you needed something and terrible if you wanted to keep a secret!"

Long before Andrew became a Methodist minister, he had a carefree life filled with nothing but play each summer in Tallahassee, Florida. "We never had a dull moment," he recalls. There were forts to construct and tear down, rocks to skip, balls to hit and throw, and of course, meals to inhale.

He is really not sure how his family managed when it came to meals. Although they were far from wealthy, there was always plenty on the table, and no one went to bed hungry.

Andrew was closest in age to his cousin Raymond, and they were inseparable. They both loved deviled eggs and frequently were reaching for the last ones on the serving platter at the end of Sunday dinner.

One Sunday after Easter in the mid-1950s, both knew there would be plenty of deviled eggs, because, after all, it was the Sunday after Easter. But for reasons Andrew can't remember, there were either fewer eggs or more eaters. Regardless, there was only one deviled egg left midway through the meal.

Both boys spied the lonely egg languishing between the pickled okra and beets they both detested. It was then that the fork battle began, with Raymond winning and instantly popping the entire egg half into his mouth. He felt the need to rub it in to Andrew and began to wax poetic about how scrumptious that last egg had been.

This made Andrew furious, and a vicious quarrel began right there at the table. Andrew's mother sent each boy to a different room to think about their horrible behavior. Their instructions were to not come out of those rooms until they could apologize. Neither boy budged.

Andrew's mother was not about to let childish pride get the best of them, so she brought a small chalkboard into each room. She encouraged each boy to write on it what he didn't want to say out loud to the other. Both wrote, "I'm sorry," and without a word, she showed each the other one's chalkboard. Then she told them they could go play, and in typical boy fashion, they acted as if nothing had ever transpired between them.

Those chalkboards came in handy several other times over the years, and while they may have had a spat over other things, a deviled egg never came between them again.

Bacon and Shrimp Deviled Eggs

A deviled egg plate should be in every Southern kitchen dish stack because it's such a classic, welcomed side dish that has universal appeal. Folding the warm bacon drippings into the yolk mixture is life changing. You can get as creative with the garnishes as you wish, but my mother and grandmother always sprinkled the tops with paprika, so I do the same.

YIELD: 6 TO 8 SERVINGS

6 large eggs

1 bacon slice

12 small cooked shrimp, finely
   chopped

1/4 cup mayonnaise

1 teaspoon Dijon mustard

1 teaspoon distilled white vinegar

1/2 teaspoon salt

1/8 teaspoon white pepper

Paprika for garnish

Place the eggs in a single layer in a saucepan and cover with water. Place over medium-high heat and just as the water comes to a boil, cover and turn off the heat. Let stand 17 minutes, then drain and run under cold water to cool. When cool enough to handle, peel and discard the shells.

Place the bacon in a medium skillet over medium-high heat. Fry for 4 minutes, turning halfway through the cooking time. Drain on paper towels and crumble when cool enough to handle. Reserve 1 tablespoon of the drippings and save any extra for another use.

Cut each egg in half lengthwise and remove the yolks to a small bowl. Arrange the whites on a serving plate. Mash the yolks with a fork and stir in the bacon drippings. Add the bacon, shrimp, mayonnaise, Dijon, vinegar, salt, and pepper. Mix well to combine. Spoon or pipe the filling equally in the egg white halves and top with a sprinkling of paprika. Chill at least 1 hour before serving.

NOTE: *If you don't have a deviled egg plate, place the halves on sprigs of fresh parsley or lettuce leaves.*

Bacon-topped Brussels Sprouts

I used to think that I didn't like Brussels sprouts, but after college I realized the error of my thinking and have been a huge fan ever since. This recipe might convert those who still avoid them. They are sautéed in a bit of bacon drippings, then cooked to perfection in a stock bath. The crumbled bacon garnish is irresistible.

YIELD: 6 SERVINGS

4 bacon slices

2 pounds Brussels sprouts,
    halved and trimmed

1/2 teaspoon onion salt

1/4 teaspoon black pepper

1 cup low-sodium chicken stock

Place the bacon in a large skillet over medium-high heat and cook until crisp, turning once. Drain on paper towels and add the Brussels sprouts to the skillet. Sprinkle with the onion salt and pepper. Cook, stirring occasionally, for 3 minutes or until the Brussels sprouts begin to soften. Add the stock, cover, and bring to a simmer. Reduce the heat to medium-low. Cook covered for 10 minutes.

Crumble the bacon. Transfer the Brussels sprouts to a serving container with a slotted spoon and garnish with the bacon pieces. Serve warm.

NOTE: *This recipe freezes well. Package, label, and freeze, then use within 3 months for the best quality.*

White Bean and Spinach Pasta Salad

I have always been a fan of pasta salads. The flavor of this dish is so different from those served warm, and the do-ahead characteristics make it a natural for Sunday dinner. This one uses common pantry and refrigerator staples to make it easy and affordable.

YIELD: 8 TO 10 SERVINGS

1 (16-ounce) package elbow macaroni

1 (16-ounce) package fresh baby spinach, coarsely chopped

1 (15-ounce) can Northern beans, drained and rinsed

1 (2-ounce) jar diced pimientos, drained

3 green onions, chopped

2 garlic cloves, peeled and minced

1/4 cup chopped dried oil-packed tomatoes

1/4 cup extra-virgin olive oil

3 tablespoons lemon juice

2 tablespoons chopped fresh oregano

1 teaspoon garlic or onion salt

1/2 teaspoon black pepper

1/4 teaspoon cayenne pepper

Shaved Parmesan for garnish

Bring a large pot of water to a boil over high heat and add the macaroni. Reduce the heat to medium and stir occasionally. Cook 8 minutes.

Place the spinach, beans, pimientos, green onions, garlic, and tomatoes in a large serving bowl. In a small bowl whisk together the olive oil, lemon juice, oregano, garlic salt, black pepper, and cayenne. Drain the pasta and immediately add to the spinach bowl. Stir gently and drizzle with the oil mixture. Garnish with the Parmesan and serve immediately, or cool slightly and serve warm or chilled.

NOTE: *To reheat refrigerated leftovers, microwave on low power rather than high.*

Summer Crowder Pea Salad

A trip to the farmers' market just got a lot more fun. This recipe is as nice with black-eye or purple hull peas. I like to serve this dish with an all-vegetable dinner or with any type of pork, thanks to the sweet fruit addition.

YIELD: 6 SERVINGS

....

3 bacon slices

3 cups cooked crowder peas

1 small red bell pepper, seeded and chopped

1/3 cup diced red onion

1/4 cup chopped fresh cilantro

1/4 cup pepper jelly

1/4 cup red wine vinegar

2 tablespoons canola oil

1 jalapeño pepper, seeded and minced

1/2 teaspoon garlic salt

1/4 teaspoon black pepper

2 large fresh peaches, apricots, or nectarines, peeled and diced

Mixed salad greens

....

Place the bacon in a large skillet over medium heat. Cook 4 minutes or until the bacon is done. Drain on paper towels and crumble when cool enough to handle. Save the drippings for another use and reserve the bacon pieces in a zip-top bag in the refrigerator until ready to serve.

In a large bowl gently stir together the peas, red peppers, and red onions. In a jar with a tight-fitting lid, combine the cilantro, jelly, red wine vinegar, oil, jalapeños, garlic salt, and black pepper. Shake vigorously to emulsify. Pour the dressing over the pea mixture, tossing to coat. Cover and chill 8 hours.

Stir the peaches into the pea mixture and set aside to come to room temperature at least 15 minutes before serving. Toss with the mixed salad greens and top with the crumbled bacon.

SUNDAY DINNER MEMORIES

Children's ministry is one of the most important areas of work in the church. Mary Ann Phillips knows this all too well. She spent decades helping establish programs for children in Methodist churches throughout the South while moving with her husband to follow his career in Mississippi, Louisiana, and finally Florida.

Mary Ann always knew she would be surrounded by kids her whole life. She quickly realized this as a young teenager when she preferred to babysit rather than hang out with her girlfriends. It came as no surprise to anyone when she dedicated her life to children's ministry.

Ask her about her favorite meal in that area of work, and she doesn't hesitate. It was back in the late 1970s when she and her husband were living in Jackson, Mississippi. She was volunteering to help with summer Bible school programs at several different churches. "My friends had the notion that once you organized one, it would be simple to repeat the process," she explained, "but it's not always that easy."

Mary Ann remembers they were nearing the end of a weeklong program when a child showed up who had not been there before. Shelby was eight years old and had walked over from the apartments that were close to the church. She carried with her a note from her mother asking if Shelby could stay for the day because she had been called in to work. After verifying the story, Mary Ann took Shelby under her wing.

The shy, reserved child soon blossomed with the other children.

It wasn't long before snack time arrived, and Mary Ann noticed that Shelby's snack was missing. She immediately replaced it, only to discover that Shelby was putting the snacks in her pockets.

Mary Ann didn't say a word, but watched as Shelby volunteered to help clean up and began stuffing her pockets with any leftover food. When she asked Shelby about it, she immediately began to cry. After much coaxing, she found out that Shelby wanted to take the food to a puppy that was left at the apartment complex.

Mary Ann grabbed some ham from the church refrigerator, loaded Shelby into her car, and went in search of the puppy that Shelby had named Rags. It didn't take long to find the little thing. They sat on the curb and fed Rags, then played with her. That's when Mary Ann knew this dog would be going home with her. For the rest of the summer, Mary Ann brought Rags over to play with Shelby each week. And Rags ended up being her companion for nearly fourteen years.

"It might seem strange that my most memorable meal was when I fed a puppy," she declares, "but that act of kindness by Shelby changed my life for the better."

Lentil and Sweet Corn Salad

I like to keep this salad on hand for quick meals all year. Serve it on mixed greens, as a side dish, or over grilled or roasted meats. It's fun to make it with lentils of any color or a mixture.

YIELD: 6 SERVINGS

1 cup lentils

1/2 cup pearl barley

1 tablespoon salt

6 tablespoons extra-virgin olive oil

2 tablespoons balsamic vinegar

2 tablespoons lemon juice

1 large garlic clove, peeled and minced

1 teaspoon onion salt

1/4 teaspoon black pepper

6 ears fresh corn, husks removed and silked

1 small red bell pepper, seeded and chopped

6 basil leaves, chopped for garnish

Bring a large stockpot of water to a boil over high heat. Add the lentils and pearl barley and cook 10 minutes. Add the salt and boil 10 minutes longer.

In a jar with a tight-fitting lid, combine the olive oil, balsamic vinegar, lemon juice, garlic, onion salt, and pepper. Shake to emulsify.

Add the corn to the boiling water and cook 5 minutes longer. Remove the corn with tongs and place on a rack to cool slightly. Drain the remaining lentil and barley mixture in a large colander. Transfer to a serving bowl and add the red peppers.

When the corn is cool enough to handle, cut the kernels from the ears. Discard the ears and place the kernels in the serving bowl and mix. Shake the dressing again and pour over the salad. Let stand 10 minutes before serving with a garnish of the chopped basil.

NOTE: *Pearl barley has had the bran layer removed, then it is steamed.*

Fresh Cranberry Molded Salad

I ate this salad years ago at my friend Thelma Barrett's home and loved it. You will fall in love all over again with gelatin salads after just one scrumptious bite. Well done, sweet Thelma!

YIELD: 6 SERVINGS

1/2 cup boiling water

1 (3-ounce) package raspberry
gelatin

2 tablespoons sugar

1 (10.5-ounce) can mandarin
oranges, drained

1/2 cup fresh cranberries

1/2 cup coarsely chopped pecans
or walnuts

1/3 cup diced celery

1/2 cup crushed pineapple,
drained with the juices
reserved

2 1/2 teaspoons lemon juice,
divided

1/4 cup mayonnaise

Lettuce leaves

In a heatproof measuring bowl, combine the boiling water, gelatin, and sugar, stirring until completely dissolved. Set aside to cool to room temperature for 20 to 30 minutes.

Place the oranges, cranberries, pecans, and celery in the bowl of a food processor. Pulse until finely chopped and stir into the gelatin mixture. Add the pineapple, 1/2 cup of the reserved juice, and 1 1/2 teaspoons of the lemon juice. Pour into 6 (1-cup) molds and refrigerate overnight.

Mix the remaining 1 teaspoon lemon juice and mayonnaise together. Cover and refrigerate until ready to serve. When ready to serve, place a lettuce leaf on each serving plate and unmold the gelatin on top. Dollop a spoonful of the lemon mayonnaise on top of each and serve.

NOTE: *Cherry gelatin can be substituted for the raspberry if desired.*

Mama's Frozen Fruit Salad

Maybe it's been awhile since you made and served this Southern classic. Maybe it's time to give it another look. There's a reason it's still popping up at mealtime, especially in the heat and humidity of the summer. This cool-me-off-in-an-instant dish can be served as a salad, side, or dessert. Green maraschino cherries will add a hint of mint flavor.

YIELD: 12 SERVINGS

1 (20-ounce) can crushed
pineapple, undrained

1 (8-ounce) package cream
cheese, softened

1 (16-ounce) jar green or red
maraschino cherries

1 (11-ounce) can mandarin
oranges, drained

1 (8-ounce) container frozen
whipped topping, thawed

2 1/2 cups miniature
marshmallows

1 cup chopped toasted pecans

1/2 cup toasted coconut

Place the pineapple and cream cheese in the bowl of a stand mixer. Drain the cherries and reserve 1/4 cup of the juice. Add the juice to the bowl and beat at medium speed for 3 minutes. Fold in the cherries, oranges, whipped topping, and marshmallows. Spread evenly in a 9 x 13-inch baking dish and top evenly with the pecans and coconut. Freeze around 3 hours or until set. Cut into squares and serve frozen.

NOTE: *You can also make this dish in single-serve portions by spooning into cupcake liners before freezing.*

SUNDAY DINNER MEMORIES

T here are parts of Virginia so poor the locals say you have to pipe in sunshine," Michael Murphy explained, "and that's where I knew God wanted me to preach." So he did, for fifty-three years, and while he admits he did not love every minute of it, he knew that's where he was supposed to be.

Michael didn't grow up in Virginia but went there on a mission trip while he was in seminary. It wasn't until after he returned that he knew he should go back; so after becoming an ordained minister, he began looking for employment opportunities that would take him there. Since there weren't a lot of people itching to go into the hills of Virginia, he found himself hired rather quickly.

"One of the most interesting things about the hill country back then was that you really didn't know which community you were in," he observed. "It wasn't organized, so you just basically went from church to church with the clothes you could carry."

This was the 1950s, and Michael questioned his wisdom more than once as he eked out a living preaching God's Word. While in one community, he was asked to visit Zack and Annie Smithson, who hadn't been seen much since Annie's mother passed away.

It took some doing, but Michael finally located their house, if you could call it that. It was more of a lean-to than anything else. He carefully knocked on the door, secretly wondering if the whole building would collapse from the activity.

Zack greeted Michael warmly and told him they were just about to have some lunch and he must join them. After exchanging pleasantries with Annie, she disappeared into what must have been the kitchen to prepare more for their unexpected guest. Michael and Zack enjoyed each other's company for just a few minutes before Annie reappeared holding a plate full of pickled eggs.

It didn't take Michael long to realize this was all they had, and he forced himself to push aside his guilt at consuming their precious commodity of food. Zack and Annie acted as though it were a four-star restaurant meal, and so did Michael. It was addictively good in its simplicity, and he thoroughly appreciated their sacrifice for him.

Later, as Michael was getting ready to leave, he realized how truly rich Zack and Annie were. They were clinging to each other for strength, and that was all that mattered. It wasn't until Michael was almost out the door that he mentioned how sorry he was about Annie's mother. That's when Annie repeated something her mother had always said and Michael has never forgotten: "You can't keep birds of sorrow from flying over your head, but you can keep them from building nests in your hair."

Southern Fried Pears

Why should apples always get the side-dish glory when pears are just as fantastic? Of course, you can use this recipe as your guide for frying apples, but switch the orange juice to lemon. Whether you peel the fruit or not is up to you. I like them unpeeled.

YIELD: 8 SERVINGS

....

3 tablespoons bacon drippings

2 tablespoons butter

6 large ripe pears, cored and sliced

2 teaspoons orange juice

1/4 cup firmly packed brown sugar*

1/8 teaspoon salt

1/8 teaspoon ground cloves

....

Place the drippings and butter in a large skillet over medium-low heat. When melted, add the pears and sprinkle with the orange juice, brown sugar, salt, and cloves. Cover and cook 15 minutes or until the pears are tender. Serve warm.

NOTE : *Anjou, Barlett, and Bosc are the best to use in this recipe. They can handle the heat and retain their shape.*

---

* You can use either light or dark brown sugar in this recipe.

Entrées

Mother's Chicken Spaghetti

This is the chicken spaghetti of my youth. Mother made this on a regular basis for us to enjoy after church. It was devoured within minutes of pulling it out of the oven. I love the memory of this dish every time I serve it, and that's always on Sunday after assembling it on Saturday. Way to go, Mother!

YIELD: 8 SERVINGS

1 whole chicken, cut up

1 large green bell pepper, seeded and chopped

1 large sweet onion, peeled and chopped

1 (4-ounce) jar diced pimientos, drained

1 (10-ounce) package thin spaghetti, broken into 4-inch pieces

2 (10-ounce) cans cream of mushroom soup

3 cups shredded sharp Cheddar cheese, divided

1 teaspoon garlic salt

1/2 teaspoon black pepper

1/4 teaspoon cayenne pepper

Place the chicken in a large Dutch oven and add enough water to cover. Place over high heat and bring to a boil. Reduce the heat to medium-low and simmer for 50 minutes.

Stir together the green peppers, onions, and pimientos in a large bowl. Lightly grease a 9 x 13-inch baking dish with cooking spray.

With tongs, remove the chicken from the cooking liquid and set aside on a rimmed baking sheet to cool slightly. With a glass 2-cup measure, scoop out 1 1/2 cups of the chicken stock and set aside. Increase the heat to high, and when the remaining liquid comes to a boil, add the spaghetti. Cook 5 to 6 minutes or until al dente. Drain in a colander placed over a bowl and add the pasta to the vegetable bowl. Cool the remaining stock and refrigerate or freeze for later use.

When cool enough to handle, pull the chicken into bite-size pieces, discarding the skin and bones. Add to the spaghetti mixture and stir in the soups and 2 cups of the Cheddar. Stir in the garlic salt, black pepper, and cayenne as well as the 1 1/2 cups reserved stock. Transfer to the prepared baking dish and top with the remaining 1 cup Cheddar.

Cover and refrigerate until ready to bake or preheat the oven to 350 degrees. Bake 40 to 45 minutes if cooking immediately or 50 to 55 minutes if refrigerated*. Let stand for 5 minutes before serving warm.

NOTE : *This casserole freezes very well. Package, label, and freeze, then use within 2 months for the best quality.*

---

* Make sure you remove the casserole from the refrigerator as soon as you begin preheating the oven, so it has time to warm up a little before you put it in the oven.

Shrimp and Sweet Pea Rice

I love serving dinners that include a bit of seafood or meat in the dish rather than as a stand-alone item. This one needs to be on a table beside sliced tomatoes, summer squash, cooked garden greens, and hot bread.

YIELD: 6 SERVINGS

....

2 tablespoons canola oil, divided

4 large eggs, lightly beaten and divided

1/4 teaspoon black pepper, divided

1/8 teaspoon salt

1 1/2 cups sliced green onions, divided

2 garlic cloves, peeled and minced

1 pound salad shrimp

5 cups cooked short-grain rice, chilled

1/4 cup low-sodium soy sauce

1/2 teaspoon onion salt

1 (10-ounce) package frozen sweet green peas, thawed

2 tablespoons chopped fresh cilantro

....

Place 2 teaspoons of the oil in a large skillet over medium-high heat. When hot, add half of the eggs and sprinkle with 1/8 teaspoon pepper and the salt. Cook 3 minutes or until the eggs are done. Remove from the pan onto a cutting board and thinly slice.

Heat the remaining 1 tablespoon plus 1 teaspoon of oil in the skillet and return to the stove. Add half of the green onions (3/4 cup) and the garlic and sauté 1 minute. Add the remaining eggs, shrimp, and rice and cook 3 minutes, stirring frequently. Add half of the reserved egg strips, the remaining 3/4 cup green onions, remaining 1/8 teaspoon pepper, soy sauce, onion salt, and peas. Cook 30 seconds, stirring constantly. Serve warm with a garnish of the remaining egg strips and cilantro, along with extra soy sauce, if desired.

NOTE: *This recipe is also good served at room temperature.*

My Favorite Chicken and Rice Casserole

This is another one of my mother's dinner masterpieces. The chicken made the rice better and vice versa. On occasion, she would prepare the chicken cooked on a bed of dressing, but the rice version was always our favorite.

YIELD: 8 SERVINGS

2 (10.75-ounce) cans cream of mushroom or cream of celery soup

2 cups low-sodium chicken stock

1 1/2 cups uncooked long-grain rice

1 teaspoon black pepper, divided

1 teaspoon paprika, divided

1/4 teaspoon cayenne pepper

1/4 teaspoon garlic powder

8 boneless skinless chicken breasts

1 tablespoon chopped fresh parsley for garnish

1 teaspoon chopped fresh chives for garnish

Preheat the oven to 375 degrees. Lightly grease a 9 x 13-inch baking dish.

In a medium bowl combine the soups, stock, rice, 1/2 teaspoon of the black pepper, 1/2 teaspoon of the paprika, cayenne, and garlic powder. Transfer to the prepared baking dish and top with the chicken. Sprinkle the remaining 1/2 teaspoon black pepper and 1/2 teaspoon paprika over the chicken.

Bake 45 to 50 minutes or until the chicken is thoroughly cooked. Let stand 10 minutes before garnishing with parsley and chives. Let the dish stand for 5 minutes before serving warm.

NOTE: *Leftovers freeze well. Package, label, and freeze, then use within 3 months for the best quality.*

Turkey and Dressing Casserole

I love Thanksgiving food and have often wondered why we save those delicious items for one time of the year. This recipe takes care of my turkey and dressing craving on any day. I make it anytime I have leftover turkey.

YIELD: 8 SERVINGS

---

4 cups chopped cooked turkey

1 (22-ounce) package frozen broccoli florets, thawed and well drained

1 (10.75-ounce) can cream of celery soup

2/3 cup sour cream

1 cup shredded Swiss cheese

1/2 teaspoon black pepper

1 (6-ounce) package stuffing mix

3/4 cup warm low-sodium chicken stock

Preheat the oven to 350 degrees. Lightly grease a 9 x 13-inch baking dish and evenly spread the turkey in the bottom. Top with the broccoli.

In a medium bowl whisk together the soup, sour cream, Swiss cheese, and pepper. Spread over the broccoli. In the same bowl combine the stuffing mix and warm stock. Sprinkle evenly over the soup layer. Bake 35 to 40 minutes or until golden brown and bubbly. Let rest 5 minutes before serving hot.

NOTE: *Leftovers freeze well. Package, label, and freeze, then use within 3 months for the best quality.*

Sunday Dinner Memories

Spending at least an hour each day studying the Bible gave Luther Fitzpatrick a great depth of knowledge and enhanced his ministry as a youth pastor. He particularly enjoyed the quiet time in the summer because the rest of his day was spent around energy-filled teenagers from his Baptist church in Tampa, Florida.

He loved starting his day with the silent reading and study time. It wasn't the only time he spent in the Bible, but it was his favorite time.

Luther realized the value of keeping young minds occupied, so he organized a summer basketball program to provide a gathering place for inner-city youth. It also gave the kids a much-needed break from the ever-present heat. Frequently, a local catering company would deliver excess items to the center, where none of it went to waste with a gym full of teenage boys around.

It was during one of those occasions that Luther sat down to talk to a boy named Toby who participated but kept to himself. Of all the donated food that was inhaled by the boys, they tended to shy away from the pickles. Toby, on the other hand, loved them and could be found nibbling on a pickle nearly every afternoon. He was doing just that when Luther collapsed next to him after running with the boys on the court.

After some small talk, the conversation turned to Bible reading, and Luther jumped at the chance to ask if Toby spent time in the Word. Toby reluctantly admitted that he spent maybe five minutes a day reading the Bible. Foolishly, Luther said that God deserved a little more of Toby's time than that and went on to brag about the hour he spent in study each morning.

Unimpressed, Toby just listened. Then, when Luther felt he had made a sufficient argument, he asked Toby if he might consider devoting more time to Bible study. Toby just said, "No."

Frustrated, Luther asked him why not, and Toby told him he felt a bit like that pickle. It took a long soak in brine to turn a cucumber into a really good pickle, and he was much the same. His time reading scriptures might be brief, but that didn't mean he didn't let it soak into him all day. He liked to let it add up and increase his knowledge bit by bit, day by day, week by week. After that, Toby was off and back on the court, while Luther was left to ponder the boy's words. He thinks of Toby every time he eats a pickle and gives him much deserved credit for showing him the wisdom of letting Scripture soak into his heart.

Kickin' Fried Chicken

This is chicken that has been dipped in a batter, then rolled in a spiced breading. Whole milk is the key, so don't try it with lower-fat versions. If any substitution is to be made, use half-and-half instead of whole milk. This chicken is amazing!

YIELD: 6 SERVINGS

5 large eggs

1 1/2 cups whole milk

4 cups all-purpose flour, divided

3 tablespoons plain cornmeal, divided

1 tablespoon baking powder

1 tablespoon plus 2 teaspoons salt, divided

2 teaspoons black pepper, divided

1 tablespoon Cajun seasoning

1 tablespoon dried thyme

1 teaspoon paprika

3 pounds bone-in chicken pieces

Vegetable oil

In a large bowl whisk together the eggs and milk for 1 minute. Add 2 cups of the flour, 2 tablespoons cornmeal, baking powder, 1 tablespoon salt, and 1 teaspoon pepper. Whisk until smooth. Let stand 15 minutes.

In a 9 x 13-inch baking dish, combine the remaining 2 cups flour, 1 tablespoon cornmeal, 2 teaspoons salt, and 1 teaspoon pepper. Stir in the Cajun seasoning, thyme, and paprika. Dip each chicken piece in the egg mixture, letting any excess drip back into the bowl. Then roll in the flour mixture, making sure to coat it well on all sides. Place on a rimmed baking sheet and continue with all the chicken. Refrigerate for 15 minutes.

Place 1 inch of oil in a large cast-iron skillet over medium heat. Clip a deep-fat thermometer to the side of the skillet, making sure the tip doesn't touch the bottom of the pan, and bring the oil to 325 degrees. Gently place just a few pieces of chicken at a time in the hot oil. Cook, turning only once, until golden brown and cooked through. This will take from 8 to 10 minutes for white meat pieces and about 12 minutes for dark meat pieces. Drain the cooked chicken on a wire rack placed over a rimmed baking sheet and repeat with the remaining pieces. Serve hot.

NOTE: *Creole seasoning or a barbecue dry rub can be substituted for the Cajun seasoning.*

Slow as a Summer Day Roasted Chicken

There is nothing finer than a perfectly roasted chicken, and if you have a good Dutch oven or a deep, large cast-iron skillet, you are halfway there. I like this one cooked on a bed of sweet onions, and the herbs add just the right touch of flavor.

Yield: 4 servings

I large sweet onion, peeled and sliced

I (4- to 5-pound) roasting chicken, giblets removed and discarded

I tablespoon coarse sea salt

I teaspoon black pepper

1/4 cup chopped fresh herbs (use a mixture of parsley, thyme, and rosemary)

2 garlic cloves, peeled and minced

2 tablespoons olive oil

Preheat the oven to 450 degrees. Lightly grease a large Dutch oven and scatter the onions on the bottom. Place the chicken on top of the onions and sprinkle all over with the salt and pepper. In a small bowl combine the herbs, garlic, and olive oil. Rub all over the chicken and place breast-side down on the onions. Roast for 15 minutes.

Reduce the oven temperature to 200 degrees and turn the chicken so that the breast side is up.* Insert a leave-in thermometer in the thigh, making sure the tip does not touch bone. Roast 4 to 5 hours or until the internal temperature reaches 170 degrees. Increase the oven temperature to 500 degrees and roast 10 minutes or until the skin is brown and crisp. Let rest 10 minutes before slicing and serving.

NOTE: *You can also use Cornish hens instead of chicken. Just watch the meat thermometer because the roasting time will be cut in half at least.*

* Turkey lifters or large tongs make turning the chicken easy.

Sweet and Sour Chicken Thighs

If you are watching your food dollars, chicken thighs should be a regular purchase at the supermarket. They are not only economical but perfectly portioned and moist, moist, moist thanks to slow cooking. You can substitute chicken wings for the thighs if desired.

YIELD: 4 TO 6 SERVINGS

. . . .

3 pounds chicken thighs

1 teaspoon coarse sea salt

1/2 teaspoon black pepper

2/3 cup low-sodium soy sauce

2/3 cup firmly packed light
brown sugar

3 garlic cloves, peeled and
minced

1 teaspoon sesame oil

1/4 teaspoon cayenne pepper

1/8 teaspoon chili powder

. . . .

Lightly grease a medium or large slow cooker. Place the chicken thighs in the bottom of the slow cooker and sprinkle with the salt and black pepper.

In a jar with a tight-fitting lid, combine the soy sauce, brown sugar, garlic, sesame oil, cayenne, and chili powder. Shake to emulsify and pour over the chicken thighs. Cover and cook on high for 4 hours or on low for 8 hours. Serve warm with the cooking liquid drizzled over the top.

NOTE: *Leftovers freeze well. Package, label, and freeze, then use within 3 months for the best quality.*

Fried Veal Cutlets

Veal is known for being tender, and this recipe practically cuts with a butter knife. But if veal is not your thing, feel free to substitute pork or chicken cutlets and you'll have an equally tasty main-dish star.

Yield: 8 servings

3 large eggs

2 cups milk

2 cups all-purpose flour

2 tablespoons plain cornmeal

1 tablespoon baking powder

1 teaspoon onion or garlic salt

1/2 teaspoon white pepper

3 cups dry seasoned bread crumbs or panko

1 tablespoon dried oregano

1 teaspoon paprika

8 (1/4-inch thick) veal cutlets, around 4 ounces each

4 tablespoons butter

2 tablespoons vegetable oil

In a medium bowl combine the eggs, milk, flour, cornmeal, baking powder, onion salt, and pepper. Set aside for 10 minutes. Place the bread crumbs, oregano, and paprika in a shallow dish. Dip each cutlet in the batter mixture, letting any excess drip back into the bowl. Then coat in the bread crumb mixture. Place on a rimmed baking sheet and refrigerate for 15 minutes.

Place the butter and oil in a large cast-iron skillet over medium-high heat. Fry the cutlets in pairs until golden brown, around 2 minutes on each side. Transfer to a wire rack over a rimmed baking sheet and repeat with the remaining cutlets. Serve warm.

NOTE: *Leftovers freeze well. Package, label, and freeze, then use within 3 months for the best quality.*

SUNDAY DINNER MEMORIES

Sleepy little towns make up for the lack of excitement with charm. Albert Pearson grew up in one of those environments and was determined to move as fast as he could to a much bigger pond. His second job with the Lutheran church was in Augusta, Georgia, and while it wasn't huge, it was growing and suited him just fine.

Danny Davis was an older gentleman who lived next door to Albert and rarely darkened the door of the church. He was a hardworking electrician who was pleasant enough, but conversations were always brief and a bit labored. So Albert was quite shocked when Danny invited him to have dinner at his house after church one Sunday. He really didn't want to go, but he accepted anyway, and then found himself dreading it all week. He scolded himself repeatedly over the attitude and tried to make himself look at it as an opportunity to get to know Danny better.

The day arrived, and Albert decided he didn't have to stay long, but he needed to go and get it over with. When he arrived at Danny's home, he was surprised that Danny had a pot roast prepared and it actually smelled quite good. Albert reached and grabbed at every piece of small talk he could muster. He had to be strategic about asking questions that could be answered with a simple yes or no because that's all he would get in return.

"I never worked so hard at talking my whole life," Albert recalls, "and it made me tired and a bit grumpy." Then Danny suggested they sit outside on the patio. There were several bird feeders hanging from the trees, and the variety of birds constantly moving among them was fascinating. That's when Danny came alive. "He told me about every bird in his yard and made it so interesting I could hardly believe this was the same man," Albert remembers. "It was remarkable!"

As Albert walked home after a terrific afternoon, he whispered a prayer of thanks for the moment and the lesson learned. He knew that Danny was far from the bore he first thought he was. And he realized that as entertaining as he thought himself to be, there must be times when he was an interesting as a tombstone. "It was life changing for me," Albert says, "and that year for my birthday he gave me a bird guide that I use to this day. We were good friends for ten years before he passed away, and I cannot see a bird without remembering him."

Roasted Brisket with Country Vegetables

This recipe can be based on the vegetables you have on hand. In the fall, switch the red potatoes out for large cubes of sweet potatoes or turnips and the carrots for parsnips. Yum!

YIELD: 8 SERVINGS

1 (4- to 5-pound) beef brisket
1 tablespoon seasoned salt
1 teaspoon white pepper
1 pound carrots, peeled and thickly sliced
1 pound small red potatoes
4 celery stalks, sliced

3 sweet onions, peeled and sliced thick
6 garlic cloves, peeled and minced
1 tablespoon chopped fresh parsley for garnish
1 teaspoon chopped fresh chives for garnish

Preheat the oven to 350 degrees. Place the brisket with the fat side down in a large roasting pan. Rub it all over with the seasoned salt and white pepper. Add enough water to come over halfway up the sides of the meat. Add the carrots, potatoes, celery, onions, and garlic around the meat. Cover tightly with foil and roast for 2 hours.

Remove and discard the foil, and with large tongs, flip the brisket so the fat side is up. If necessary, add more water to make sure it is over halfway up the sides of the meat. Continue cooking at least 4 hours longer until the meat is browned and fork-tender.

Transfer to a cutting board with a liquid moat. Let it rest 10 to 15 minutes. Strain the drippings into a gravy bowl, reserving the vegetables. Slice the meat against the grain on the diagonal into 1/2-inch thick slices. Transfer to a serving platter and surround with the vegetables. Garnish with the parsley and chives. Serve with the pan drippings on the side.

NOTE: *Leftovers freeze well. Package, label, and freeze, then use within 3 months for the best quality.*

Oven-Braised Short Ribs

Long, slow, moist cooking is a necessity for short ribs to tenderize properly. The carrots become irresistibly soft and flavorful, as do the onions, making an instant vegetable side dish.

YIELD: 6 TO 8 SERVINGS

3 tablespoons vegetable oil

3 tablespoons butter

I tablespoon plus I teaspoon salt, divided

I tablespoon paprika

2 1/2 teaspoons black pepper, divided

6 pounds bone-in beef short ribs

I pound carrots, peeled, cut into large slices, and divided

6 celery stalks, sliced and divided

2 sweet onions, peeled and coarsely chopped

6 garlic cloves, peeled and minced

I (28-ounce) can whole tomatoes, undrained

4 cups low-sodium beef stock

1/2 cup chopped fresh parsley

I teaspoon chopped fresh thyme

Preheat the oven to 350 degrees. Place the oil and butter in a large Dutch oven over medium-high heat. In a small bowl mix together 1 tablespoon salt, paprika, and 2 teaspoons pepper. Rub all over the ribs and add to the Dutch oven. Brown on both sides for around 2 minutes and transfer to a platter. Brown in batches, if necessary.

Add half of the carrots and celery to the Dutch oven, as well as the onions and the remaining 1 teaspoon salt and 1/2 teaspoon pepper. Cook, stirring occasionally, for 5 minutes. Add the garlic and cook 3 minutes longer. Return the ribs to the pot and add the tomatoes and their juices as well as the stock, parsley, and thyme. Bring to a boil, cover, and transfer to the oven. Cook 1 1/2 hours.

Stir in the remaining carrots and celery, cover, and return to the oven to cook for 1 1/2 hours longer. Serve warm.

NOTE: *Leftovers freeze well. Package, label, and freeze, then use within 3 months for the best quality.*

Ham and Greens Pot Pie with Cornbread Crust

This one-dish meal is nothing short of Southern fine. It incorporates everything we call soul food, and the mixture is magic. Serve this in warmed soup bowls with tablespoons so you don't miss any of the incredible juices.

YIELD: 8 TO 10 SERVINGS

2 tablespoons vegetable oil

4 cups chopped cooked ham

3 tablespoons plus 1/2 cup all-purpose flour, divided

3 cups low-sodium chicken stock

1 (16-ounce) package frozen mixed vegetables, thawed and drained

1 (16-ounce) package frozen chopped kale or turnip greens, thawed and squeezed dry

1/2 teaspoon crushed red pepper flakes

1 1/2 cups plain cornmeal

2 teaspoons baking powder

1/2 teaspoon salt

2 large eggs, lightly beaten

1 1/2 cups buttermilk

4 tablespoons butter, melted

Preheat the oven to 425 degrees. Lightly grease a 9 x 13-inch baking dish. Place the oil in a Dutch oven over medium-high heat. Add the ham and sauté 4 to 5 minutes or until lightly browned. Sprinkle evenly with 3 tablespoons flour and cook 1 minute longer, stirring constantly. Gradually add the stock and bring to a boil. Cook 3 minutes, stirring constantly.

Add the mixed vegetables and kale and return to a boil. Cook 5 minutes, stirring frequently. Add the red pepper flakes and transfer to the prepared baking dish.

In a medium bowl combine the cornmeal, remaining 1/2 cup flour, baking powder, and salt. Make a well in the center and add the eggs, buttermilk, and melted butter. Stir until just moistened. Pour evenly over the ham mixture. Bake 23 to 25 minutes or until the cornbread is golden brown. Serve warm.

NOTE: *This recipe benefits from resting for 5 minutes after removing from the oven.*

Spring Vegetable and Ham Strata

Refrigeration is a requirement of this recipe, which makes it an excellent after-church meal. Do the assembly first thing Sunday morning, then it's ready to pop in the oven upon your return from church. Leftovers reheat beautifully.

YIELD: 8 SERVINGS

4 cups water

2 cups asparagus spears, trimmed and cut into 2-inch pieces, divided

3 cups French bread cubes, divided

2 cups shredded Gruyere cheese

1/2 cup chopped sweet onions

1/4 cup chopped green onions, green parts only

2 1/2 cups cooked diced ham, divided

10 large eggs, divided

1 1/2 cups milk or half-and-half

1/2 teaspoon garlic salt

1/4 teaspoon black pepper

1/4 teaspoon paprika

In a large pan over high heat, bring the water to a boil. Add the asparagus and cook 4 to 5 minutes or until tender. Drain and plunge immediately into a bowl of ice water. Leave for 4 minutes, drain again, and set aside to cool slightly.

Lightly grease a 3-quart baking dish and cover the bottom with 2 1/2 cups bread cubes. Top with the Gruyere, sweet onions, green onions, half of the ham, and half of the asparagus, in that order. Then top with the remaining 2 1/2 cups bread crumbs.

In a small bowl whisk together 4 of the eggs, milk, garlic salt, pepper, and paprika until well blended. Pour evenly over the layers in the baking dish. Press down the bread pieces with the back of a wooden spoon. Top with the remaining ham and asparagus. Cover and refrigerate for 1 hour or up to 4 hours.

Preheat the oven to 325 degrees. Bake uncovered for 30 minutes. With the back of a wooden spoon, press 6 indentations into the top of the strata. Crack one whole

egg and place into an indentation. Repeat with the remaining eggs. Bake 25 more minutes or until the eggs are set. Remove from the oven and place on a wire rack. Let stand for 15 minutes before cutting into squares and serving warm.

Brown Sugared Ham

This recipe makes good use of ginger ale rather than dark cola, and the difference is quite noticeable. It is still sweet but in a more delicate way, and the leftovers are remarkable between slices of mayonnaise spread on fresh soft white bread.

YIELD: 10 TO 12 SERVINGS

1 (9-pound) smoked bone-in ham (ready to cook and trimmed)

2 (12-ounce) bottles ginger ale or lemon-lime soda

1/4 cup firmly packed dark brown sugar

1 1/2 teaspoons black pepper

1/2 teaspoon salt

1/2 teaspoon dry mustard

1/4 teaspoon paprika

Preheat the oven to 325 degrees. Lightly grease a large roasting pan.

Make shallow diamond-shaped cuts in the fat of the ham. Place the ham with the fat side up in the prepared roasting pan. Add the ginger ale to the pan and loosely cover with heavy-duty aluminum foil. Bake 4 to 4 1/2 hours or until a meat thermometer inserted in the thickest part registers 140 degrees.

In a small bowl stir together the brown sugar, pepper, salt, dry mustard, and paprika. Remove the ham from the oven and uncover. With thick plastic gloves, sprinkle the brown sugar mixture over the ham, pressing into the fat as much as possible. Bake uncovered another 20 to 25 minutes or until the sugar crust is browned and a meat thermometer registers 145 degrees. Remove from the oven and let stand 15 minutes before transferring to a cutting board and carving. Serve warm.

NOTE: *Leftovers freeze well. Package, label, and freeze, then use within 3 months for the best quality.*

Sausage and Beef Meatloaf

I have never met a meatloaf that didn't taste better the following day. That means you can serve one loaf and send the other home with your dinner guests or make it ahead of time and reheat it for some serious meatloaf munching madness!

YIELD: 2 LOAVES (12 TO 14 SERVINGS)

1 pound hot ground pork sausage

1 pound ground chuck or ground sirloin

1 (15-ounce) can tomato sauce

1 green bell pepper, seeded and diced

1 large shallot, peeled and diced

1 sleeve saltine crackers, crushed

2 large eggs, lightly beaten

Preheat the oven to 425 degrees. Line the bottom and sides of 2 loaf pans with aluminum foil, allowing at least 2 inches to extend over the sides. Fold the foil down along the sides of the pan and lightly grease the inside.

In a large bowl gently combine the sausage, ground chuck, tomato sauce, green peppers, shallots, crackers, and eggs. Divide the mixture evenly into the 2 prepared loaf pans. Bake 50 minutes or until a meat thermometer inserted in the center registers 160 degrees. Let stand 10 minutes before removing from the pans, using the foil sides as a handle. Slice and serve warm.

NOTE: *If using only one loaf, let the remaining loaf cool completely in the pan. Wrap in heavy-duty aluminum foil or freezer paper, label, and freeze up to one month.*

Sunday Dinner Memories

Eugene Duncan loves Sunday dinner. He admits that it's the perfect way for clergy to relax after morning services. Although he is now retired from the Presbyterian church, he relished invitations from his congregation and rarely had to decline due to conflicts. He appreciated the effort and sacrifice made to have him as a guest in their homes.

Billy and Jo Beth Finley issued one of those invitations, and Eugene readily accepted. They had a large family with nine children and were in the pews practically every time the church doors opened.

Jo Beth was a renowned cook in the community, and that only added to the enthusiasm Eugene had for the upcoming meal.

Recently, the family had experienced a series of hardships, and they were finally coming out on the other side. Eugene was grateful they found a reason to celebrate.

Eugene arrived right on time at the spacious yet simple farmhouse they owned. It wasn't fancy by any means, but was situated on land that had been in Billy's family for decades. The smell of something fried hit Eugene as soon as he walked in the front door, and his mouth immediately began to water.

Eugene and Billy enjoyed a cold beverage in the den as the final preparations were made for dinner. It took some wrangling on Billy's part, but everyone found a seat at the spacious farm table that seemed to take up most of the house.

Naturally, Billy asked Eugene to bless the food. As he started the blessing, he realized how much this family had endured and felt the need to recognize the struggles and their victory. Then something came over him. "I suppose I just got carried away," he says, "and I didn't mean to, but obviously I continued to pray much longer than I had intended or the family wanted."

Eventually, Eugene said, "Amen," to which Jeb, their oldest boy, responded, "And, Lord, please bring down fire to warm our now cold food!" At first no one moved or uttered a word. Then Eugene erupted in laughter that was soon contagious to everyone at the table.

They went on to enjoy a terrific fried chicken meal, but Eugene got much more from the experience than a full belly. He learned to keep it quick when there's chicken on the table!

Smothered Lamb Chops

Thick-cut lamb chops are elegant and seem extravagant. It's a reason to become friends with your supermarket butcher. They are kept juicy with an easy-to-prepare foolproof gravy enhanced with mushrooms and onions.

Yield: 6 servings

2 tablespoons vegetable oil, divided

6 thick-cut lamb chops (2 pounds)

1/2 teaspoon salt

1/4 teaspoon black pepper

1/4 teaspoon white pepper

1 3/4 cups low-sodium vegetable stock

2 tablespoons cornstarch

1 sweet onion, peeled and thinly sliced

1 cup sliced fresh mushrooms

2 garlic cloves, peeled and minced

Place 1 tablespoon of the oil in a very large skillet over medium high heat. Sprinkle the lamb evenly with the salt, black pepper, and white pepper. Add to the skillet and cook 3 minutes on each side. In a small bowl whisk together the stock and cornstarch until completely smooth.

Remove the lamb from the skillet and set aside to drain on paper towels. Add the remaining 1 tablespoon oil to the skillet. When hot, add the onions and cook 4 minutes, stirring occasionally. Add the mushrooms and garlic and cook another 2 minutes. Stir in the reserved stock mixture and bring to a boil, stirring constantly. Cook 5 minutes or until the mixture thickens.

Return the lamb to the skillet and reduce the heat to low. Cover and cook an additional 5 minutes or until the lamb is cooked through. Serve warm with a generous helping of the gravy.

NOTE: *Leftovers freeze well. Package, label, and freeze, then use within 3 months for the best quality.*

Sour Cream Mushroom Chicken

Think of this as beef stroganoff without the beef. The chicken substitute gives you a lighter version of the meal that is spring-like but with the same fantastic creamy gravy.

Yield: 4 to 6 servings

2 tablespoons canola or vegetable oil

1 tablespoon butter

1 sweet onion, peeled and diced

1 (8-ounce) package fresh sliced mushrooms

4 to 6 boneless, skinless chicken breasts

1 tablespoon paprika

1 small red bell pepper, seeded and chopped

1/2 cup low-sodium chicken stock

2 teaspoons garlic salt

3 tablespoons sour cream, room temperature

3 tablespoons heavy cream or half-and-half, room temperature

Cooked egg noodles

2 tablespoons chopped fresh parsley for garnish

Place the oil and butter in a large skillet over medium heat. When the butter melts, add the onions and mushrooms and sauté 4 minutes. Add the chicken and sprinkle with the paprika. Cover and cook 10 minutes.

Add the red peppers, stock, and garlic salt and reduce the heat to low. Cover and cook 45 minutes or until the chicken is completely done. Just before serving, stir together the sour cream and cream in a small bowl and add to the chicken mixture. Serve over hot cooked egg noodles and garnish with the parsley.

Shrimp and Wild Mushroom Casserole

I have used all sorts of seafood in this recipe, and I encourage you to do the same. Make a switch to anything you have on hand to give it a new spin. If you don't have shrimp, use clams, scallops, or crabmeat.

YIELD: 10 TO 12 SERVINGS

3 cups long-grain and wild rice

4 tablespoons butter, divided

1 sweet onion, peeled and chopped

1 (4-ounce) package sliced wild mushrooms

2 (10.75-ounce) cans cream of mushroom or cream of shrimp soup

1/2 cup low-sodium chicken stock

1 tablespoon lemon juice

1 tablespoon Worcestershire sauce

1/4 teaspoon black pepper

2 pounds small or medium cooked shrimp, peeled and deveined

1 cup dry plain bread crumbs or panko

2 tablespoons grated Parmesan cheese

Cook the rice according to the package directions. Preheat the oven to 350 degrees. Lightly grease a 9 x 13-inch baking dish.

Place 2 tablespoons of the butter in a large skillet over medium-high heat. When melted, add the onions and mushrooms and sauté 6 to 7 minutes. In a large bowl stir together the soups, stock, lemon juice, Worcestershire, and pepper. Add the onion mixture, cooked rice, and shrimp. Gently mix and spread in the prepared baking dish.

Add the remaining 2 tablespoons butter to the skillet and melt over low heat. Stir in the bread crumbs and toss to evenly coat. Remove from the heat and stir in the Parmesan. Sprinkle evenly over the shrimp mixture. Bake 30 minutes or until the topping is golden brown. Let rest 5 minutes before serving warm.

NOTE: *Leftovers freeze well. Package, label, and freeze, then use within 2 months for the best quality.*

Sunday Dinner Memories

David Leach is a traveling man; he's been in ministry throughout the South. His infectious laughter is contagious and oozes
from his spirit. Even though his ministry is now centered around
San Antonio, Texas, he goes back to days spent in Nicholasville,
Kentucky, when recounting a great Sunday meal.

Do you remember a TV show from the 1970s called *The Waltons*?
Well, that's what it was like when you were a guest in the home of John
and Betty Carpenter. In addition to their family of six, you also found
yourself in the company of numerous relatives on any given Sunday,
with everyone crammed around a big oak table in the Carpenters'
comfortable kitchen.

The meal spread before you was more than a feast. This was the
kind of meal where table legs groaned from the weight of all the
plentiful food piled from one end to the other. It was country cooking at its finest, and every dish was equally rich and delectable.

During Dave's first meal in the Carpenters' home, he saw these
roundish, flat cornbread-looking things that reminded him of the way
bluegill was prepared and fried when he was growing up in Indiana.
Naturally he jumped to the conclusion that fish was exactly what was
being served and eagerly asked for the bluegill.

A hush fell over the room, and all he got back was blank stare
after blank stare. No one had a clue what Dave was asking for. Finally

someone realized he was talking about the deep-fried corn fritters and hilarity ensued. But instead of being embarrassed, Dave laughed along with them and ended up changing the language of that entire family. They were never called corn fritters again at the Carpenters'. From that moment on, the fritters were known as bluegill, and always with a round of hearty laughter.

Spinach and White Bean Chicken

Fresh spinach is such a terrific ingredient. It cooks up fast, looks great, and is loaded with vitamins and minerals that elevate it to nutritional powerhouse status. It tops this balsamic vinegar—basted chicken with panache!

YIELD: 4 SERVINGS

2 tablespoons canola oil

4 boneless, skinless chicken breasts

1/4 teaspoon black pepper

3 garlic cloves, peeled and minced

1/3 cup balsamic vinegar

1 (10.75-ounce) can condensed golden mushroom soup

1 (15-ounce) can cannellini beans, drained and rinsed

1 (8-ounce) bag fresh baby spinach

1/4 cup coarsely chopped pecans, toasted

Place the oil in a large skillet over medium-high heat. Sprinkle the chicken with the pepper and add to the hot skillet. Cook 5 minutes on each side and drain on paper towels. Add the garlic and cook 1 minute, stirring frequently.

Stir in the balsamic vinegar and cook 1 minute longer, scraping up any bits that have stuck to the bottom of the skillet. Add the soup and beans and bring to a boil. Reduce the heat to medium and return the chicken to the skillet. Top with the spinach and cover. Cook 10 to 12 minutes longer or until the chicken is no longer pink. Top with the pecans and serve warm.

NOTE: *Leftovers freeze well. Package, label, and freeze, then use within 4 months for the best quality.*

Cracker-topped Seafood Casserole

If you are a fan of seafood, you'll love this creamy combination of shrimp and crabmeat. It is topped off with a buttery cracker crust that provides a nice crunch against the luscious seafood. Feel free to substitute scallops or crawfish if you wish.

YIELD: 6 SERVINGS

1 pound medium shrimp, peeled and deveined

1 (10-ounce) package frozen chopped spinach, thawed and squeezed dry

2 (6-ounce) cans lump crabmeat, drained

1 (10.75-ounce) can cream of shrimp soup

3 garlic cloves, peeled and minced

2 green onions, sliced

1/2 cup mayonnaise

1/4 teaspoon black pepper

1/4 teaspoon cayenne pepper

1/4 teaspoon paprika

1 sleeve butter-flavored crackers, crushed

2 tablespoons butter, melted

Preheat the oven to 350 degrees. Lightly grease a 2-quart baking dish. Layer the shrimp, spinach, and crabmeat in the baking dish. In a medium bowl whisk together the soup, garlic, green onions, mayonnaise, black pepper, cayenne, and paprika. Spread over the top of the crabmeat. Top evenly with the cracker crumbs and drizzle with the butter. Bake 30 minutes or until hot and bubbly. Let stand 5 minutes before serving warm.

NOTE: *Leftovers freeze well. Package, label, and freeze, then use within 2 months for the best quality.*

Baked Chicken Ranch

Here is a recipe that demonstrates how delicious boneless, skinless chicken breasts can be, and it's done in less than 30 minutes.

YIELD: 6 TO 8 SERVINGS

....

8 boneless skinless chicken
  breasts
1 teaspoon salt
1/2 teaspoon black pepper
2/3 cup ranch-style dressing

1/3 cup Dijon mustard
1/4 cup firmly packed brown
  sugar*
Hot cooked rice

....

Preheat the oven to 350 degrees. Lightly grease a 9 x 13-inch baking dish and add the chicken making sure it is in a single layer. Sprinkle evenly with the salt and pepper.

In a medium bowl whisk together the ranch dressing, Dijon, and brown sugar until smooth. Pour over the chicken and spread to evenly coat. Bake 25 minutes or until the chicken is cooked. Serve warm over hot cooked rice.

---

* You can use either light or dark brown sugar in this recipe.

Sunday Dinner Memories

Wallace Williams declares he has preached longer than many people have lived. "I started preaching when I was sixteen years old, and I'm ninety-one and still going strong," he says. Even though he is officially retired, he continues to preach to anyone he sees because "God is in my blood!"

He has a razor-sharp mind and recalls a great meal back in 1978 at the home of Martha Grant, a lively Sunday school teacher at the Mission Church in L.A. (lower Alabama).

Martha was known to rescue any cat that managed to make it to the city limits. So when she insisted that Wallace and his new wife, Thelma, come for Sunday dinner, he felt the need to warn his bride about the possibility of cat contact. Neither of them liked cats, but it was decided they could handle it and agreed to be at her home by one thirty after church.

Nothing could have prepared them for the amount of cats at her home! There were cats all over the yard and cats appearing from secret hiding places, eager to greet them as Wallace and Thelma emerged from their car. Their legs were encircled by cats of every size and color, all wanting attention. Immediately, Thelma told Wallace she had lost her appetite, and he did too. He begged her to try as best as she could, with the pep talk being as much for him as for her.

Martha yelled for them to come on in as soon as they knocked on her door. To their surprise, her home was spotless, without a cat in sight. But they were both leery, expecting some paws to appear from underneath the sofa at any moment.

They enjoyed a meal of fresh vegetables and cornbread without a meow heard during the feast. By the time they had coffee and angel food cake in the den, they had completely relaxed and realized there were no cats inside. After a marvelous visit, Wallace and Thelma headed home, scolding themselves for the preconceived ideas of cats being everywhere, including inside.

It wasn't until they changed clothes to relax for the rest of the afternoon that they saw it . . . cat hair was all over the backs of their clothes. It wasn't just a few hairs here and there, but everywhere! "To this day, I don't know where those cats were, or if the ones we saw in the yard had been moved there from inside," he says with a chuckle. "But we learned that looks can be very deceiving!"

T-Squared Turkey and Tomato Casserole

I love using turkey tenderloins. They are such a nice change from chicken, and the extra stock you get from the preparation is sensational. You can make this dish ahead of time and refrigerate until ready to bake. Just add another ten minutes to the baking time as it will go from the refrigerator to the oven.

YIELD: 8 SERVINGS

2 turkey tenderloins (5 pounds total)

2 celery stalks, cut into large pieces

2 carrots, peeled and cut into large pieces

3 teaspoons seasoned salt

2 tablespoons butter

1 sweet onion, peeled and chopped

1 green bell pepper, seeded and chopped

1 garlic clove, peeled and minced

2 (10.75-ounce) cans cream of mushroom or cream of celery soup

2 (10-ounce) cans diced tomatoes with green chilies, drained

1 teaspoon dried oregano

1 teaspoon ground cumin

1 teaspoon chili powder

2 cups shredded Gruyere cheese, divided

Place the turkey, celery, carrots, and seasoned salt in a large Dutch oven and cover with water. Place over medium-high heat and bring to a boil. Reduce heat to low, cover, and simmer 45 minutes. Remove the Dutch oven from the heat and then remove the turkey from the stock. Let cool 45 minutes.

Strain the remaining stock and reserve 1 cup. Refrigerate or freeze the rest of the stock for another use. Melt the butter in the same Dutch oven over medium-high heat. Add the onions and sauté 6 minutes. Add the green peppers and garlic and sauté 4 minutes longer.

Preheat the oven to 350 degrees. Lightly grease a 9 x 13-inch baking dish. Stir the reserved 1 cup of stock, cream of mushroom soup, diced tomatoes with green chilies, oregano, cumin, and chili powder into the skillet. Cook 8 minutes, stirring occasionally.

Cut the turkey into bite-size pieces and place half into the prepared baking dish. Cover with half of the soup mixture and 1 cup Gruyere. Repeat the layers, ending with remaining 1 cup cheese. Bake 55 minutes or until bubbly. Let stand 10 minutes before serving warm.

NOTE: *Leftovers freeze well. Package, label, and freeze, then use within 4 months for the best quality.*

Hickory Grilled Flank Steak

Overnight marinating is the key to making this cut of beef fork-tender. It needs just the right combination of oil and acid to break down the tough fibers, and this concoction fills the bill. This meat is perfect alongside a green salad or any green vegetable.

YIELD: 6 SERVINGS

....

1 (3-pound) flank steak

1/3 cup vegetable oil

1/4 cup red wine vinegar

1 tablespoon liquid smoke

1/2 teaspoon garlic powder

1/2 teaspoon black pepper

....

Place the flank steak in a large, heavy-duty zip-top bag. In a jar with a tight-fitting lid, combine the oil, red wine vinegar, liquid smoke, garlic powder, and pepper. Shake well to emulsify and pour over the steak. Seal the bag, place on a large plate, and refrigerate 8 hours or overnight.

Bring the meat to room temperature for 20 minutes. Preheat the grill to medium-high (375 degrees to 400 degrees). Remove the steak from the marinade and discard the marinade. Place the steak on the grill, close the lid, and cook for 8 to 9 minutes. Turn and cook another 8 to 9 minutes for medium, or to the desired degree of doneness. Only turn the meat once, leaving it to cook undisturbed. Remove to a cutting board with a moat. Let rest 10 minutes, then cut into thin slices across the grain and serve warm.

NOTE: *You can substitute skirt steak for the flank steak if desired.*

Sunday Dinner Memories

Elizabeth Geitz is like a cool breeze on a warm summer day. She makes you comfortable, relaxed, and in the mood to recline and listen to her perfect Southern accent. She has retained it in spite of being transplanted in the North for the past few decades. Listening to her talk is like hearing a mockingbird sing.

As an ordained Episcopal priest, Elizabeth understands compassion and discovered her passion in the most unlikely of places. This Vanderbilt graduate unearthed her true mission in life nestled in the country of Cameroon, West Africa.

If you put it on paper, her connection there would look like a drawing from the late 1960s toy called Spirograph. It's a wiggly, circular path that dips and curves all over the place and demonstrates how frequently God indirectly guides us to where we need to be.

The year was 2008, and Elizabeth was the sponsor of a child at the Good Shepherd Home Orphanage in Cameroon. She had corresponded with him for several years when Elizabeth decided it was time for the two to meet. It wasn't long before she was on the plane, then taking an eight-hour bus ride to the orphanage with three other friends.

When they arrived, Elizabeth and the others were greeted as genuinely and enthusiastically as humanly possible. There was dancing, clapping, singing, and plenty of hugging to go around. On the second day, the women were measured. They weren't sure why, but wondering was lost in the myriad things to do.

The evening before they departed, the friends were presented exquisite handmade African dresses. After changing into this precious gift, they were escorted to three little plastic chairs that were placed on a rug and were handed bouquets of handpicked greens. Then there was dancing, singing, and music performed for their honored guests. At some point in the festivities, corn was popped, which was a real treat for the children. They dined like queens on a feast of chicken, rice, cooked greens, and wine.

Even now, Elizabeth is humbled by the hospitality she was shown from brothers and sisters in Christ who have little more than that to give. In Africa, they have a beautiful word, *ubuntu*, which means "I in you and you in me." It underlines their unselfish actions of sharing all they have. Just about the time you expect they have given everything, they give and give again. What they gave Elizabeth was more than a meal and more than a cherished gown. They gave her a glimpse of the face of God and how He shines no matter what the circumstance.

(For more information on how you can help the Good Shepherd Home children, go to http://www.goodshepherdsustainability.org.)

Cajun Crawfish Casserole

This dish is as colorful as the area of the South it celebrates. An added plus is that leftovers freeze well. If you don't care for crawfish, feel free to substitute shrimp. If you're a fan of both crawfish and shrimp, use a mixture of the two to really impress.

Yield: 6 servings

4 tablespoons butter

1 small sweet onion, peeled and chopped

1/2 cup chopped red bell pepper

1/2 cup chopped yellow bell pepper

1/2 cup chopped green bell pepper

4 garlic cloves, peeled and minced

2 cups fresh or frozen sliced okra

1 tablespoon lemon juice

1 1/2 teaspoons salt

2 pounds crawfish tails

3 cups cooked long-grain rice

1 (10.75-ounce) can cream of shrimp soup

1/2 cup milk or half-and-half

1 tablespoon low-sodium soy sauce

1/2 teaspoon cayenne pepper

1/4 cup grated Parmesan cheese

Preheat the oven to 375 degrees. Lightly grease an 11 x 7-inch baking dish.

Place the butter in a large skillet over medium-high heat. Add the onions, red peppers, yellow peppers, and green peppers. Sauté 7 minutes, stirring occasionally. Add the garlic and sauté 1 minute longer. Stir in the okra, lemon juice, and salt. Sauté 5 minutes, stirring occasionally.

Add the crawfish, rice, soup, milk, soy sauce, and cayenne, stirring well to combine. Transfer to the prepared baking dish and sprinkle evenly with the Parmesan. Bake 17 to 20 minutes or until bubbly. Let stand 5 minutes before serving warm.

NOTE: *Use refrigerated leftovers within 2 days.*

Honey Mustard Pork Chops

This is a recipe that I keep returning to because it's deceptively simple and turns out perfect each and every time. You can dust the outside with any fresh herbs you have on hand. Serve the chops with creamy mashed potatoes and hot buttered rolls.

YIELD: 6 SERVINGS

6 (3/4-inch thick) bone-in pork chops

1 teaspoon garlic or onion salt

1/2 teaspoon black pepper

6 tablespoons butter, softened

1/4 cup fresh chopped parsley (or fresh herb of your choice)

3 tablespoons honey mustard*

Preheat the broiler on high. Grease a wire rack and place over a rimmed baking sheet. Put the pork chops on the wire rack. Sprinkle evenly with the garlic salt and pepper. In a small bowl stir together the butter, parsley, and honey mustard. Place a heaping tablespoon of the butter mixture on top of each chop.

Broil 10 minutes or until an instant-read thermometer reads 155 degrees when inserted in the center. Let rest 5 minutes before serving hot.

---

* If you have no honey mustard on hand, mix 1 teaspoon of honey with enough regular mustard to make 3 tablespoons.

Peppercorn Strip Steaks

Start with whole spices that you crush with a mortar and pestle. Then rub it on the steaks for an explosion of spiced flavor. All this needs is a green salad and the bread of your choosing.

YIELD: 4 SERVINGS

1 teaspoon dill seeds
1 heaping teaspoon black
    peppercorns

1 teaspoon coriander seeds
1 1/2 teaspoons coarse salt
4 (1 1/2-inch thick) strip steaks*

Place the dill seeds, peppercorns, and coriander seeds in a mortar and grind coarsely with a pestle. Add the salt and mix well with your fingers. Rub the spice blend evenly over the steaks.

Preheat the grill to medium-high. Grill to your desired degree of doneness, but turn the meat only once. Around 8 minutes total will give you medium-rare steaks. Let rest 5 minutes before serving warm.

---

* You will sometimes see strip steak labeled at Delmonico or New York steak.

Mustard-Smeared Roasted Pork Shoulder

This is a great make-ahead recipe. It slow-roasts in the oven the day before you need it. Then it can be served any way you want. I like it over a bed of creamy, hot grits. Leftovers make great sandwiches for Monday's lunch.

YIELD: **8** SERVINGS

....

1 (5 1/2-pound) pork shoulder

3 garlic cloves, peeled and minced

1/2 cup Dijon mustard

2 tablespoons chopped fresh sage

2 tablespoons chopped fresh parsley

1 tablespoon honey or sorghum syrup

1/2 teaspoon kosher salt

1/4 teaspoon black pepper

Hot sauce

....

Preheat the oven to 225 degrees. Lightly grease the rack of a roasting pan and place the pork on the rack, fat side up. In a small bowl combine the garlic, Dijon, sage, parsley, honey, salt, and pepper. Use your hands to spread the rub all over the pork. Roast 9 hours or until the pork is well browned and very tender. Let the meat rest at least 15 minutes before pulling apart and serving warm with a dribble of hot sauce.

NOTE: *You can substitute honey mustard for the Dijon if desired.*

Sunday Dinner Memories

The Lutheran church has been a vital part of Donald Armstrong's life for as long as he can remember. Growing up in North Carolina, he loved going to church. "I especially remember a fabulous stained glass window I always wanted to sit near," he recalls. "I liked watching how the sun would stream through it and reflect various colors on my hymnal."

It was no surprise to anyone when Donald decided to devote his life to ministry. He soon settled in Greensboro and knew he was in a community he adored. Over the years, he became friends with Herbert Trent, who was the custodian for the church. Herbert was a happy worker who seemed to be constantly whistling a snappy tune that remained stuck in your head for the rest of the day. He was a little slow to accomplish things, but extremely thorough and a joy to be around.

Donald was surprised when Herbert asked him to be his dinner guest one Sunday, but cheerfully accepted. Then Herbert said that Donald needed to change into really comfortable clothes before he came over, which he was happy to do.

Donald was right on time for dinner and was met by a beaming Herbert. He had two fishing poles, a tackle box, and a cooler already sitting on the front porch, ready to load into Herbert's vehicle. Instantly, Donald understood why he was told to be in comfortable clothes.

The afternoon was spent eating peanut butter and banana sand-wiches and fishing at Herbert's favorite spot. They drank ice-cold Cokes from eight-ounce glass bottles and topped them off with oatmeal cookies. It was the finest meal Donald ever enjoyed. "We caught some mighty fine fish and kept the date at least every month when the weather was right and the fish were biting," he said. "The meal was always the same . . . and it was perfect!"

Balsamic-Glazed Pork Steaks

Pork steaks are usually cut from the shoulder but can also come from the loin. They are thick and a good alternative to beef when cooking for a crowd. They can be smoked, broiled, baked, or grilled, as they are in this recipe. Make the balsamic glaze the day before if you have time issues.

YIELD: 4 SERVINGS

---

1 cup balsamic vinegar
1/4 cup firmly packed brown
   sugar*

4 pork steaks
1 teaspoon garlic or onion salt
1/2 teaspoon black pepper

Place the balsamic vinegar and brown sugar in a small saucepan over medium heat, stirring constantly until the sugar dissolves. As soon as the mixture comes to a boil, reduce the heat to low and cook for about 15 minutes or until the mixture thickens and coats the back of a spoon.

Preheat the grill to medium-high. Sprinkle the steaks evenly with the garlic salt and pepper on both sides. Grill 7 minutes on each side. Brush the glaze on each steak during the final minute of cooking. Serve warm.

* You can use either light or dark brown sugar in this recipe.

Roasted Pork Tenderloin with Apricot Glaze

A sweet sauce always seems to make pork better. This recipe utilizes your oven for the tenderloin, then you can quickly prepare the glaze on the stovetop while the meat is resting.

YIELD: 8 SERVINGS

2 (2-pound) pork tenderloins

2 tablespoons olive oil

1 tablespoon chopped fresh thyme

2 teaspoons sugar

1 teaspoon kosher salt

1/2 teaspoon black pepper

1 cup apricot preserves

1/2 cup apple cider or apple juice

1 tablespoon cider vinegar

Preheat the oven to 400 degrees. Lightly grease a rimmed baking sheet. Place tenderloins close together on the baking sheet and rub with the olive oil. In a small bowl combine the thyme, sugar, salt, and pepper. Sprinkle evenly over the tenderloins. Insert a meat thermometer in one of the tenderloins about halfway through the center and place in the oven so the dial can be seen from the oven window. Roast for 25 minutes or until the thermometer reads 165 degrees. Remove the pan from the oven and let the tenderloins rest for 10 minutes before removing to a cutting board with a moat for slicing.

In a saucepan over medium heat, combine the preserves, apple cider, and cider vinegar. Cook, whisking constantly, for 8 minutes. Drizzle the glaze over the pork slices and serve warm.

NOTE: *You can substitute peach preserves for the apricot if desired.*

Frosted Sweet Potato Cake (page 261)

Desserts

Warm Strawberry Cobbler

Strawberries always seem to get shortchanged in the cobbler area in favor of shortbread. No more! I love the rustic way this dish is prepared and served in a cast-iron skillet. You will too.

YIELD: 8 SERVINGS

2 pints fresh strawberries, hulled
  and sliced

3/4 cup sugar, divided

2 tablespoons lemon juice

1 tablespoon cornstarch

1 cup all-purpose flour

1 cup plain cornmeal

2 tablespoons baking powder

Pinch of salt

6 tablespoons cold butter, cut
  into pieces

1 large egg

1/2 cup half-and-half

Fresh whipped cream

In a medium bowl combine the strawberries, 1/4 cup of the sugar, lemon juice, and cornstarch. Let stand 15 minutes.

Preheat the oven to 375 degrees. Grease a 10-inch cast-iron skillet.

In a bowl whisk together the flour, cornmeal, remaining 1/2 cup of sugar, baking powder, and salt. Add the butter and cut into the flour mixture with a pastry blender or 2 forks until the butter is incorporated. In a small bowl whisk together the egg and half-and-half. Stir the egg mixture into the flour mixture. Place the strawberry mixture into the prepared skillet. Drop batter by spoonsful on top of the strawberries. Bake 30 to 35 minutes, or until golden brown. Remove from the oven and let cool at least 15 minutes before serving with dollops of whipped cream.

No-Bake Strawberry Pie with Chocolate Crust

Make-ahead desserts are always necessary when having guests into your home for dinner. This one is just as cool as it is sophisticated, and there is no need to heat up the kitchen by turning on the oven.

YIELD: 8 SERVINGS

25 chocolate wafer cookies

3 ounces bittersweet chocolate, melted

2 teaspoons vegetable oil

1 (8-ounce) package cream cheese, softened

1/3 cup powdered sugar

3/4 teaspoon pure vanilla extract

2 cups frozen whipped topping, thawed

1 pint fresh strawberries, hulled and cut into wedges

2 tablespoons strawberry jam

1/2 teaspoon lemon juice

Place the cookies in the bowl of a food processor and process until finely ground. Add the melted chocolate and oil and process until well combined. Press into a 9-inch pie plate, making sure the crust evenly covers the bottom and up the sides. Place in the freezer for 15 minutes.

In the bowl of an electric mixer, combine the cream cheese, powdered sugar, and vanilla until smooth, about 2 minutes. Fold in the whipped topping and carefully spread over the crust. Top evenly with the strawberries.

Place the jam in a small glass bowl and microwave on high power for 10 seconds. Stir in the lemon juice and whisk until smooth. Drizzle over the strawberries. Chill at least 30 to 45 minutes before slicing and serving.

NOTE: *As the fruit season changes, substitute fresh raspberries for the strawberries and raspberry jam for the strawberry jam.*

Icebox Cookies

What could be better than a crisp sugar cookie? The serving possibilities are endless. You can crumble them over homemade ice cream, serve them with fresh peach slices, or just munch on them alone. The dough can be made ahead of time, then just sliced and baked when needed.

YIELD: 8 DOZEN COOKIES

....

1 1/2 cups white sugar

1 cup (2 sticks) butter, softened

1/2 cup firmly packed light
   brown sugar

1 tablespoon pure almond extract

2 large eggs

3 1/2 cups all-purpose flour

1/2 teaspoon baking soda

1/2 teaspoon salt

....

Place the white sugar, butter, brown sugar, and almond extract in the bowl of an electric mixer and beat at medium speed for 2 minutes. Reduce the mixer speed to low and add the eggs one at a time, beating just until the eggs are incorporated.

In a medium bowl stir together the flour, baking soda, and salt. Add to the butter mixture gradually, beating at low speed just until it is blended. Transfer the dough to a cutting board and divide into 4 equal portions. Shape each portion into a log that is roughly 2 inches in diameter. Wrap each log in plastic wrap and refrigerate at least 8 hours and up to 4 days.

Preheat the oven to 350 degrees. Cut each log into thin (around 1/4-inch) slices and place on parchment-lined baking sheets. Bake 10 to 12 minutes or until lightly browned around the edges. Immediately transfer to wire racks to cool. Store in airtight containers.

VARIATION: *Sprinkle the tops with finely chopped almonds, cinnamon sugar, assorted cookie sprinkles, or colored sugar before baking.*

Sunday Dinner Memories

Having meat during a weekday meal was rare at the Jefferson house in Raleigh, North Carolina. With a tightly stretched food budget, you could expect it on the table at the Sunday dinner meal, but not any other time.

Randall Jefferson continued to practice that habit while serving as a missionary through the Lutheran church. It helped him exist on the meager salary he received. He laughs as he tells me about his granddaughter having "Meatless Mondays" at her house. He chuckles when he says, "We had Meatless Mondays, Tuesdays, Wednesdays, Thursdays, Fridays, and Saturdays at our house!"

When talking about special meals, he remembers one in particular, and not surprisingly it involved meat in a Sunday meal. It was getting close to the holidays in 1971 when Randall's grandmother came for a visit. She brought all the supplies to make a new meal called "Hamburger Helper," and everyone was anxious to give it a try after church on Sunday.

Randall recalls it being incredible and was well into his second helping when his sister Addie was asked about her week in school. Never one to be shy, Addie started bragging about having the highest grades in her class. It wasn't just a passing comment. She went on and on about how brilliant she was while Randall rolled his eyes and continued to enjoy his newfound hamburger love.

Randall's father excused himself from the table for a minute and returned with a balloon in his hand. While Addie was in mid-sentence, still telling everyone how smart she was, Mr. Jefferson started blowing up the balloon. That got everyone's attention!

Mr. Jefferson named the balloon Elmer and started telling about all the fantastic things that Elmer did. With each equally magnificent act, he blew up the balloon just a little more, holding it right next to Addie. The bigger Elmer got, the more Addie tried to move away from the balloon, knowing it was going to pop at any moment.

Then Mr. Jefferson asked a question: "It isn't much fun to be around Elmer anymore, is it?" Everyone, including Randall's grandmother, said that it wasn't. Then he told Addie, "That's the way anyone feels when they are around someone with a big head."

It was a lesson that has stayed with Randall his whole life, and he is still reminded of it every time he sees a package of Hamburger Helper. Well played, Mr. Jefferson. Well played!

Strawberry Lemon Squares

I have been making these dessert bars for eons, and I never get tired of them. They have an extra bonus of traveling well if you are having dinner on the grounds. They can be served without the garnish if you are taking them to another location.

Yield: 12 to 15 servings

....

2 cups all-purpose flour

1/2 cup powdered sugar

3/4 teaspoon lemon zest, divided

3/4 cup (1 1/2 sticks) cold butter, cut into cubes

2 (8-ounce) packages cream cheese, softened

3/4 cup white sugar

2 large eggs

1 tablespoon lemon juice

1 cup strawberry preserves

2 cups whipped cream

1 pint fresh strawberries, washed

....

Preheat the oven to 350 degrees. Lightly grease a 9 x 13-inch baking dish.

In a medium bowl combine the flour, powdered sugar, and 1/2 teaspoon of the lemon zest. Cut in the butter with a pastry blender or 2 forks until crumbly. Press into the bottom of the prepared dish and bake 20 minutes or until lightly browned.

Place the cream cheese and white sugar in the bowl of an electric mixer. Beat at medium speed until smooth, about 2 minutes. Add the eggs one at a time and blend until smooth. Stir in the lemon juice and remaining 1/4 teaspoon zest.

Spread the preserves evenly over the warm crust and top with the cream cheese mixture. Bake an additional 30 minutes or until set. Cool on a wire rack for 1 hour. Cover and refrigerate at least 4 hours.

When ready to serve, cut into squares and top with a dollop of whipped cream and a whole quartered strawberry.

SUNDAY DINNER MEMORIES

Timothy Hughes did not grow up in the South, but has claimed it as his home of choice after travels all around the world. He distinctly remembers when he knew he would become a priest in the Catholic church.

It was on a trip to southern Ireland when he was just a boy. In a church the family visited, all the windows were stained glass except for one that had a spectacular view of a crystal-blue lake against a backdrop of green mountains. Underneath the window it read, "The heavens declare the glory of God and the firmament showeth His handiwork."

"That stopped me in my tracks," Father Tim recalls, "and I knew at that second my life would be dedicated to God." That he found his way eventually to Georgia seems a little surreal to him now. He is retired and living with his nephew in Atlanta, but has no trouble recalling the best meal he enjoyed as a priest.

It was a blustery day in early January during the 1980s, and Father Tim was feeling very over-socialized after the holiday season. He just wanted to "burrow in my cave," and relished the silence it brought with it.

But eighty-seven-year-old Mary Ruth Simpson would hear nothing of it. She insisted that Father Tim come to her home for Sunday dinner and would not let it go. He eventually relented, and she sent her driver to pick him up after mass.

He was thrilled to learn that it would be just the two of them for dinner because he was not in the mood for the larger crowd he expected. Then, rather than taking him to the grand entrance of her palatial home, the driver took him around to the back of the property to the horse barn. When he entered, it was all he could do not to gasp. Inside was an enormous, beautifully lit fireplace with two cushioned Adirondack chairs facing the fire. The back doors were open to reveal a breathtaking view of the hillside.

Mary Ruth greeted him with wine and escorted him to the chairs. Unbelievable to him even now, they roasted hot dogs and marshmallows while enjoying what looked like a canvas painting in front of them. It was the perfect prescription for a weary soul. They talked about nothing in particular, and the afternoon revived his soul.

The following year she died, and her service was held in that barn and attended by a select few friends whom she knew would appreciate the surroundings. As they toasted her, Father Tim couldn't help but give heaven a little wink because he knew she was entertaining in heaven the way only the epitome of a Southern lady could.

Grilled S'more Bananas

Dessert doesn't have to be complicated, and this recipe proves it. The grill has this recipe ready to serve in less than ten minutes. Plan for more than one per person to be on the safe side or you'll leave them wanting more!

YIELD: 6 SERVINGS

8 bananas

1/2 cup miniature chocolate chips

1/2 cup miniature marshmallows

1/4 cup chopped pecans

Preheat the grill to medium. Leave the bananas in their skins and make a slit down the length of the banana without cutting it in half. Stuff each banana with the chocolate chips and marshmallows. Wrap each banana in heavy-duty aluminum foil and place on the grill away from direct heat. Grill 6 to 8 minutes. Remove from the grill and carefully open each foil packet. Sprinkle with the pecans and serve warm in the foil wrapping.

NOTE: *You can also cook this in a 350-degree oven for 6 to 8 minutes.*

White Chocolate Cheesecake

I have always been a fan of white chocolate. I think it's the surprise you get from having it not immediately recognized in recipes. It's subtle, but noticeable at the same time. I like how it is showcased in this dessert with the added bonus that the dish can be made ahead of time.

YIELD: 10 TO 12 SERVINGS

12 to 14 thin almond cookies

6 (1-ounce) squares white chocolate, coarsely chopped

1 (8-ounce) package cream cheese, softened

1/2 cup heavy cream

1/4 teaspoon pure almond extract

1/3 cup semisweet chocolate chips

Line an 8-inch baking pan with aluminum foil. Place the almond cookies in a single layer along the bottom of the pan.

Place the white chocolate in a glass bowl and microwave on low power for 30 seconds. Stir and repeat the microwaving process until completely melted. In the bowl of an electric mixer, beat the cream cheese at medium speed until light and fluffy, about 2 minutes. Add the melted white chocolate, cream, and almond extract. Beat until smooth and spread over the almond cookies.

Cover and refrigerate at least 2 hours or until set. Place the semisweet chocolate chips in a small glass bowl and microwave on low power for 30 seconds. Stir until smooth. Slice and serve the cheesecake with a drizzle of warm chocolate.

Lemon Cream with Fresh Blueberries

Luscious fresh blueberries are topped with a tangy whipped cream that can be made the day before. It is equally incredible with fresh blackberries, strawberries, or even chilled seedless grapes.

YIELD: 4 TO 6 SERVINGS

1/2 cup heavy cream

1 tablespoon powdered sugar

1/4 cup lemon curd

1 pint fresh blueberries, washed and drained

1 teaspoon grated lemon zest

4 to 6 mint sprigs

Place the cream and powdered sugar in the bowl of an electric mixer and beat at high speed for 3 minutes or until soft peaks form. Fold in the lemon curd. Cover and refrigerate until ready to serve. Also place 4 to 6 individual serving bowls in the refrigerator to chill.

Place the blueberries in the chilled bowls and top with a generous garnish of the lemon cream. Sprinkle with the zest and top with a mint sprig. Serve immediately.

NOTE: *You will find lemon curd on the jam and jelly aisle of the supermarket.*

Ralph the parakeet ended up sitting on Jimmy Dale's shoulder throughout the entire meal, and Dan is still not sure how he managed to remain composed. He just kept asking the Lord to please keep that bird on Jimmy Dale's shoulder and not let it attack him. God answered that prayer!

Much to Dan's relief, Mae suggested they have dessert on the terrace, where Dan says he thoroughly enjoyed two slices of what he now calls "Ralph-free" raspberry jam cake. Awards go to Mae Roberts for her great jam cake and to Dan Shoemake for getting through life without a single parakeet scratch on him!

Swirled Chocolate Cake with Chocolate Velvet Frosting

This is the dessert to make when you want the meal to end in a **wow!** *I love the visual punch provided by this cake that is laced with swirls of yellow and chocolate batter. And the buttery, smooth frosting recipe that follows is pure decadence.*

YIELD: 14 TO 16 SERVINGS

....

1 cup (2 sticks) butter, softened

2 1/4 cups sugar

1 2/3 cups milk, room temperature

1 cup heavy cream, room temperature

1 tablespoon pure vanilla extract

3 cups all-purpose or cake flour

1 tablespoon baking powder

1 teaspoon salt

6 large eggs, separated

1/2 teaspoon cream of tartar

6 (1-ounce) squares bittersweet chocolate, melted

1/4 cup boiling water

1/4 teaspoon baking soda

Chocolate Velvet Frosting (recipe follows)

....

Preheat the oven to 350 degrees. Grease and flour 3 (9-inch) round baking pans.

In the bowl of an electric mixer, cream the butter at medium-high speed for 2 minutes. Gradually add the sugar and beat another 2 minutes.

In a medium bowl combine the milk, cream, and vanilla. In a separate medium bowl combine the flour, baking powder, and salt. Add the egg yolks, one at a time, to the butter mixture, beating well after each addition. Reduce the mixer speed to low and beginning and ending with the flour mixture, alternately add flour mixture and milk mixture to the butter mixture.

In another bowl of an electric mixer, beat the egg whites and cream of tartar on high speed until stiff peaks form, about 3 minutes. Gently fold into the batter. Do not mix until smooth. Some egg white pieces should be visible.

In another medium bowl combine the melted chocolate, boiling water, and baking soda. Place 1 cup of the batter into the chocolate mixture and blend well.

Evenly divide the remaining batter into the prepared pans and smooth to the edges. Spoon 1/3 heaping cup of the chocolate mixture in a large strip on top of the cake batter in each pan. With a table knife cut through the layers, swirling the batter to create a marbled effect.

Bake 30 to 35 minutes or until a tester inserted in the center of each layer comes out with moist crumbs. Remove from the oven and place each pan on a wire rack to cool for 10 minutes. Remove the layers from the pan to cool completely before frosting.

To frost, place a heaping cup of Chocolate Velvet Frosting on the top of the bottom cake layer. Spread evenly and top with another layer. Spread another heaping cup of frosting evenly over that layer. Top with the final layer and repeat with another heaping cup of frosting. Frost the sides, and use any extra frosting on the top. Refrigerate until an hour or so before slicing and serving.

Chocolate Velvet Frosting

The last thing you want to do is not have enough frosting. No fear of that here, so feel free to pile it high!

YIELD: 6 CUPS

2 1/4 cups butter, softened

6 cups powdered sugar

1/2 teaspoon salt

2 tablespoons corn syrup

2 tablespoons unsweetened cocoa powder

1 tablespoon plus 1 1/2 teaspoons pure vanilla extract

1 (16-ounce) package bittersweet chocolate, melted and cooled

5 tablespoons heavy cream, divided

Place the butter in the bowl of an electric mixer and beat at high speed for 2 minutes. In a medium bowl combine the powdered sugar and salt.

Reduce the mixer speed to medium and add the corn syrup, cocoa powder, and vanilla. Fold in the melted chocolate. Reduce the mixer speed to low and add half of the powdered sugar mixture. Add 3 tablespoons of the cream, then the remaining powdered sugar mixture, and the remaining 2 tablespoons cream. Use immediately to frost a completely cooled cake.

Cocoa Clouds

These are not your typical end-of-the-meal cookies. They seem to be part candy and dissolve in your mouth with rich chocolate that lingers deliciously on the tongue.

YIELD: 3 DOZEN COOKIES

2 large egg whites

1/2 teaspoon pure vanilla extract

1/8 teaspoon cream of tartar

2/3 cup sugar

1 tablespoon unsweetened cocoa

1/2 cup mini semi-sweet or milk chocolate chips

Line two baking sheets with parchment paper and preheat the oven to 300 degrees.

In the bowl of an electric mixer, beat the egg whites on high speed until soft peaks form, about 2 minutes. Add the vanilla and cream of tartar and continue mixing at high speed for 30 seconds. Add the sugar 2 tablespoons at a time. Add the cocoa and fold in the chocolate chips.

Drop rounded tablespoons onto the prepared baking sheets, making sure they are 2 inches apart. Bake for 20 minutes or until the bottoms are lightly browned. Transfer to a wire rack to cool completely before serving. Store in an airtight container.

Chocolate Hickory Nut Pie

This pie needs to be cut in small slices because it is fabulously rich. So rather than a usual eight slices from a pie, you'll get nearly a dozen delicious servings. The buttery hickory nuts are excellently spotlighted here.

YIELD: 10 TO 12 SERVINGS

1 Food Processor Piecrust
  (page 227)
1/2 cup sugar
1/3 cup all-purpose flour
Pinch of salt
2 large eggs, lightly beaten

1/2 cup sorghum or dark corn
  syrup
1 teaspoon pure vanilla extract
1 cup chopped hickory nuts
4 (1-ounce) squares semisweet
  chocolate, finely chopped
3/4 cup (1 1/2 sticks) butter,
  melted

Prepare the piecrust according to the directions, making sure to refrigerate the prepared crust for 1 hour. Preheat the oven to 375 degrees. Fill the crust with pie weights and bake 15 minutes or until the edges are barely golden brown. Remove the pie weights and continue baking another 10 minutes. Place on a wire rack and cool for at least 50 minutes or until completely cool.

Preheat the oven to 350 degrees. In a large bowl stir together the sugar, flour, and salt. Add the eggs, corn syrup, vanilla, nuts, and chocolate. Add the melted butter and stir until well combined. Transfer to the cooled crust and bake 35 minutes until the pie is set but still a little soft. Cool at least 1 hour on a wire rack before slicing and serving.

NOTE: *You can substitute chopped walnuts or pecans for the hickory nuts if desired.*

Cranberry Nut Fudge

Fudge is a great homemade candy to serve after a heavy meal because a small piece is all that's necessary. And this fudge is deliciously easy to make and is perfect for the holidays.

YIELD: 48 PIECES

12 (1-ounce) pieces white chocolate

3/4 cup sweetened condensed milk

1 cup coarsely chopped almonds, toasted

1/2 cup dried cranberries

Line an 8-inch square baking pan with foil, making sure the foil extends over the sides of the pan by 2 inches.

Place the chocolate and condensed milk in a glass bowl and microwave on medium power for 3 minutes or until the chocolate is almost melted. Stir until the mixture is smooth and add the almonds and cranberries. Blend well. Spread evenly into the prepared pan. Refrigerate at least 2 hours or until firm.

Lift the fudge out of the pan using the foil edges as a handle. Cut into squares and serve immediately or store in an airtight container in the refrigerator up to 3 weeks.

NOTE: *You can substitute chopped dried cherries for the cranberries if desired.*

Frosted Fudge Brownies

Brownies that have a layer of frosting on the top immediately seem a bit fancier than those that are missing that extra bit of sweetness. And of course they are richer and more decadent as well!

Yield: 24 brownies

---

1 cup (2 sticks) butter, softened

3 (1-ounce) squares semisweet chocolate, melted

3 large eggs

2 cups white sugar

3 teaspoons pure vanilla extract, divided

1 cup all-purpose flour

1 cup chopped pecans or walnuts

3 cups miniature marshmallows

1/2 cup (1 stick) butter, melted

3 1/4 cups powdered sugar

6 tablespoons unsweetened cocoa

6 tablespoons milk

Preheat the oven to 325 degrees and lightly grease a 9 x 13-inch baking dish.

Place the 1 cup softened butter, melted chocolate, eggs, white sugar, 2 teaspoons of the vanilla, and flour in a large bowl and stir until smooth. Fold in the pecans. Evenly spread into the prepared baking dish and bake 30 to 35 minutes or until the edges pull away from the pan. Place on a wire cooling rack and immediately top with the marshmallows, pressing into the brownies. Cool completely.

In the bowl of an electric mixer, combine the 1/2 cup melted butter, powdered sugar, cocoa, milk, and the remaining 1 teaspoon vanilla. Beat 10 to 12 minutes or until smooth. Spread over the top of the cooled brownies. Cut and serve.

NOTE: *Place leftovers in an airtight container and store either at room temperature or in the refrigerator.*

Brown Sugar Sour Cream Cake

This feather-light dessert can be made ahead, but find a hiding place out of sight from your family. They will be more than tempted to cut a slice after smelling it bake!

YIELD: 12 SERVINGS

1 cup (2 sticks) butter, divided

2 cups firmly packed light brown sugar, divided

2 large eggs

1 cup sour cream

1 teaspoon pure vanilla extract

2 3/4 cups all-purpose flour, divided

1 tablespoon baking powder

2 teaspoons ground cinnamon, divided

1/2 teaspoon baking soda

1/2 teaspoon salt

2 cups chopped pecans, divided

Remove 1/2 cup of the butter from the refrigerator and allow it to soften. Preheat the oven to 350 degrees. Lightly grease a 9-inch square or 11 x 7-inch baking pan. In the bowl of an electric mixer, beat the softened butter and 1 cup of the brown sugar at medium speed until light and fluffy, about 3 minutes. Add the eggs one at a time, blending well after each addition. Fold in the sour cream and vanilla.

In a medium bowl whisk together 1 cup of the flour, baking powder, 1 teaspoon cinnamon, baking soda, and salt. Add to the butter mixture mixing at low speed until blended. Stir in 1 cup of the pecans and spread evenly into the prepared pan.

In the bowl used for the flour mixture, whisk together the remaining 1 3/4 cups flour, 1 cup brown sugar, and 1 teaspoon cinnamon. Cut the remaining 1/2 cup cold butter into the flour mixture with a pastry blender or 2 forks. Stir in the remaining 1 cup pecans and sprinkle on top of the cake batter.

Bake 50 minutes or until a tester inserted in the center comes out clean. Cool completely in the pan on a wire rack before cutting into squares and serving.

Grapefruit Meringue Pie

Clouds of fluffy meringue enhance nearly any pie, but they are especially delightful over a sweet, tangy filling based on grapefruit juice that is exceptional.

YIELD: 8 SERVINGS

5 large eggs, separated

2 (14-ounce) cans sweetened
   condensed milk

1/3 cup grapefruit juice

1 (9-inch) graham cracker crust

1/2 teaspoon cream of tartar

1 cup sugar

Preheat the oven to 350 degrees. In the bowl of an electric mixer, beat the egg yolks at high speed for 2 minutes. Reduce the speed to medium-low and add the condensed milk and grapefruit juice. Spoon into the graham cracker crust and bake 15 minutes.

Remove the pie from the oven and place on a wire rack. Place the egg whites and cream of tartar in the bowl of the electric mixer and beat at high speed until soft peaks form, about 2 minutes. Gradually add the sugar 1 tablespoon at a time, mixing until stiff peaks form.

Very lightly score the baked filling with a fork in vertical lines. Spoon the meringue in a circle along the pie edge, making sure to completely seal against the pie edge. Spoon the remaining meringue in the center, making decorative swirls. Bake 10 minutes or until the top of the meringue lightly browns. Cool to room temperature on a wire rack and then refrigerate until ready to slice and serve.

Like every other child on the planet, a trip home from school ignites the stomach, and hunger pangs were racing as the brothers galloped into the house. Snacks, snacks, snacks! They must have snacks or they would surely die! As their mother poured glasses of milk, they eagerly anticipated the arrival of those remaining éclairs. But much to their surprise, she only pulled out one, saying that she had put the other one in their father's lunch.

She put a knife next to the éclair on the plate and said, "One of you divide it and the other has first choice." Larry quickly grabbed the knife and started to divide the éclair unequally. Then he realized the significance of his mother's words and cut the éclair in exact halves.

As he recounts the story now, he still knows that box of chocolate éclairs was the best ever made. And he also knows he learned a valuable lesson on how to share.

Flourless Chocolate Cake with Hazelnuts

Cakes that are prepared without flour are rich, gooey, and dense, so serve small slices.

Yield: 12 servings

12 (1-ounce) squares bittersweet chocolate, chopped

3/4 cup (1 1/2 sticks) butter, cut into pieces

6 large eggs

1 cup firmly packed light brown sugar

1/2 cup hazelnut liqueur, divided

1 cup finely ground hazelnuts

1 teaspoon kosher salt

1 cup heavy cream

Chopped toasted hazelnuts

Preheat the oven to 350 degrees. Grease and line the bottom of a 9-inch springform pan with parchment paper. Wrap the outside of the pan tightly with 3 layers of heavy-duty aluminum foil. Place in a large roasting pan.

Place the chocolate and butter in the top of a double boiler or a small bowl set over a saucepan of simmering water. Whisk until the mixture is melted, then remove the bowl from the heat. Set aside to cool slightly.

In a medium bowl combine the eggs, brown sugar, and 1/4 cup of the hazelnut liqueur with a whisk until well blended. Add the chocolate mixture and whisk until smooth. Stir in the hazelnuts and salt. Transfer to the prepared pan.

Pour enough hot water into the roasting pan to come halfway up the sides of the springform pan. Place in the center of the oven and tent the roasting pan loosely with foil. Bake 1 1/2 hours or until the cake is set. Remove the springform pan from the roasting pan and the foil from around the pan and cool completely on a wire rack. Chill for 2 hours.

Just before serving, beat the remaining 1/4 cup hazelnut liqueur and the heavy cream in the bowl of an electric mixer until soft peaks form, about 2 minutes. Run a knife along the inside of the pan to loosen the cake and release the sides. Top slices with the whipped cream and a sprinkling of chopped nuts.

Buttermilk Jam Cake

This recipe is dessert perfection. The tang of buttermilk, the just-right spices, and lusciously sweet jam are joined together in an incredible old-fashioned cake. Use any kind of jam you have on hand. I change it to fit the season.

YIELD: 12 SERVINGS

1 cup buttermilk

1 teaspoon baking soda

1 cup (2 sticks) butter, softened

2 cups white sugar

4 large eggs, room temperature

1 teaspoon pure vanilla extract

3 cups all-purpose flour

1 1/2 teaspoons ground cinnamon

1 teaspoon ground allspice

3/4 teaspoon ground cloves

1/2 teaspoon salt

1 (18-ounce) jar strawberry, raspberry, or seedless blackberry jam

1 cup finely chopped toasted pecans

Powdered sugar for garnish

Preheat the oven to 350 degrees. Grease and flour a 10-inch tube pan.

In a small bowl combine the buttermilk and baking soda. In the bowl of an electric mixer, beat the butter at medium speed until creamy, around 2 minutes. Gradually add the white sugar and beat until light and fluffy, about 2 minutes longer. Add the eggs one at a time, beating just until incorporated. Stir in the vanilla. In a medium bowl combine the flour, cinnamon, allspice, cloves, and salt.

Beginning with the flour mixture, add to the butter mixture gradually and alternate with the buttermilk mixture. Beat on low speed just until blended after each addition. Add the preserves and beat until just blended. Stir in the pecans. Transfer the batter to the prepared pan.

Bake 65 to 70 minutes or until a tester inserted in the center comes out clean. Cool in the pan for 10 minutes, then remove to a wire rack to cool completely, around 1 1/2 hours. When ready to slice and serve, dust with powdered sugar.

Peach Crumb Pie

Crumb toppings on pies are less intimidating for new cooks and seem a little more casual than two-crust versions. I have substituted other fruits in this pie, but keep returning to peaches.

YIELD: 8 SERVINGS

1 Food Processor Piecrust
  (page 227)

2/3 plus 3/4 cup white sugar,
  divided

1/3 cup firmly packed light brown
  sugar

2 tablespoons plus 3/4 cup all-
  purpose flour, divided

1 tablespoon quick-cooking
  tapioca

1 teaspoon ground cinnamon

1/2 teaspoon salt, divided

6 cups sliced fresh peaches

1/2 teaspoon pure vanilla extract

6 tablespoons cold butter, cut
  into pieces and divided

1 teaspoon baking powder

Preheat the oven to 375 degrees. Place the piecrust in a 9-inch pie dish and flute the edges. Place the crust in the freezer.

In a medium bowl stir together 2/3 cup of the white sugar, brown sugar, 2 tablespoons of the flour, tapioca, cinnamon, and 1/4 teaspoon of the salt. Add the peaches and gently toss to evenly coat. Drizzle with the vanilla and spoon into the piecrust. Dot with 2 tablespoons of the cold butter. Bake 8 minutes and remove from the oven. Lower the oven temperature to 350 degrees.

In a medium bowl mix together the baking powder and the remaining 3/4 cup flour, 3/4 cup white sugar, and 1/4 teaspoon salt. Using a pastry blender or 2 forks, cut in the remaining 4 tablespoons butter until the mixture is crumbly. Spread evenly over the peach filling and bake 35 to 40 minutes. If the top begins to over-brown, cover with foil. Cool completely on a wire rack before slicing and serving.

Grilled Fresh Pineapple with Coconut Lime Drizzle

When you get your first taste of fresh pineapple that comes off the grill, you'll find many reasons to duplicate the effort. This recipe is basic in technique and scrumptious in flavor. And when served while fresh pineapple is in season, it is inexpensive as well.

YIELD: 6 SERVINGS

1 large pineapple, peeled, cored, and cut into bite-size pieces

1/2 cup sweetened coconut flakes

1 lime

2 tablespoons firmly packed light brown sugar

1 tablespoon butter

Preheat the grill to medium and lightly grease a grilling basket. Place the pineapple pieces in a single layer in the basket. Grill about 8 minutes, turning once halfway through.

Place the coconut under the broiler on high and toast for 1 minute or until lightly browned. Zest the lime and sprinkle over the coconut.

Juice the lime into a small bowl and add the brown sugar and butter. Microwave on low power for 1 minute and stir to combine until the butter is melted. Transfer the grilled pineapple to a serving bowl and drizzle with the lime juice mixture. Sprinkle the top with the zest and coconut and serve warm.

SUNDAY DINNER MEMORIES

When Maxwell Jones first began preaching in the mid-1960s, he was anxious to immerse himself into the everyday lives of his newly formed church. Atlanta, Georgia, was not the metropolitan city it is today, so navigating through what was then a town was easy. To save money, he lived with his brother, Everett, and his family. Maxwell's five-year-old niece, Natalie, whom he called Nat, had the key to his heart.

Maxwell had been on the job all of two weeks when he received a call from Mable Boatright. She was in charge of the local cake-baking contest at the fair and asked if he would be a judge. Maxwell said yes before he really thought about it because the idea of getting to taste all those delicious cakes was so tempting. "At the time, I weighed about 130 pounds soaking wet," he remembered, "and I could put away some cake!"

The day of the contest arrived. There were true works of art on display. Maxwell tasted what seemed like every kind of cake imaginable. He soon realized that this job was going to be harder than he originally thought. A little over halfway through the entries, he was beginning to feel the effects of taking too many bites. But he continued on, and a stellar, fresh coconut cake was the blue-ribbon winner.

After having his picture taken for the local newspaper, all Maxwell could think of was how quickly he could get home and lay on the couch. He didn't want another piece of cake again for a very long time.

He arrived back at Everett's house to a sea of activity with chores being done and dinner being prepared. He said he didn't want a thing and went straight to the couch to recuperate from his afternoon indulgence. He was nearly asleep when he felt a small tug on his sleeve. Opening one eye, he saw little Nat standing there smiling from ear to ear.

Maxwell sat up and gave his cherished niece a hug, and she said she had made a surprise for him. She could hardly contain her excitement as she asked if he was ready for it. After the obligatory closing of the eyes and counting to ten, Maxwell opened his eyes to see a beaming Nat holding something behind her back. Then she presented him with a delight she had made in her Easy-Bake Oven . . . a cake!

Maxwell mustered all the inner fortitude he had to sit and eat that delicious cake with Nat. And even though he had tasted some mighty fine creations that afternoon, the best was a tiny cake baked under a lightbulb served by a very proud five-year-old.

Chocolate Orange Tarts

These individual tarts have a surprising hint of orange that makes them extra special. Thanks to the mixing time, the filling puffs up while it bakes, then charmingly falls as the tarts cool.

Yield: 12 servings

2 (2.75-ounce) packages high-quality chocolate bars

6 tablespoons butter

2 large eggs

2 large egg yolks

1/2 cup sugar

2 tablespoons finely grated orange zest

1/4 teaspoon salt

1 tablespoon all-purpose flour

12 partially baked mini pie shells

Place the chocolate and butter in the top of a double boiler or a small metal bowl set over a saucepan of water over medium-high heat. Cook over simmering water, stirring frequently, until the chocolate has melted. Remove from the heat and set aside to cool for 10 minutes, stirring occasionally.

Preheat the oven to 350 degrees. In the bowl of an electric mixer with the whisk attachment, combine the eggs, egg yolks, sugar, orange zest, and salt at medium-high speed. Mix for 6 minutes.

Reduce the mixer speed to low and sprinkle the flour over the egg mixture. Fold in the chocolate mixture and gently mix until combined.

Evenly spoon the chocolate mixture into the mini pie shells and place on a rimmed baking sheet. Bake 14 to 15 minutes. Cool on a wire rack before serving.

Three Milk Sponge Cake

Beaten egg whites give this cake a very light, airy texture that is moistened with a mixture of sweetened milk. The end result is simply impossible to resist.

YIELD: 12 SERVINGS

5 large eggs, separated

1 cup all-purpose flour

1 1/2 teaspoons baking powder

1/4 teaspoon salt

1 cup white sugar, divided

1/3 cup milk

1/2 teaspoon pure vanilla extract

1/2 teaspoon pure almond extract

1 (14-ounce) can sweetened condensed milk

1 (13-ounce) can evaporated milk

2 1/4 cups heavy cream, divided

3 tablespoons powdered sugar

Preheat the oven to 350 degrees. Lightly grease a 9 x 13-inch baking dish. Place the egg whites in the bowl of an electric mixer and beat on high speed until soft peaks form, about 2 minutes.

In a medium bowl stir together the flour, baking powder, salt, and 3/4 cup of the white sugar. When soft peaks form on the egg whites, gradually add the remaining 1/4 cup white sugar and continue beating until stiff peaks form again, another 1 to 2 minutes.

In a large bowl whisk the egg yolks for 1 minute until beaten. Add the milk, vanilla extract, and almond extract. Stir into the flour mixture and thoroughly combine. Fold in the beaten egg whites and spread evenly in the prepared baking dish.

Bake 35 to 45 minutes or until a tester inserted in the center comes out clean. Turn the cake onto a platter that is rimmed and cool completely.

Combine the condensed milk, evaporated milk, and 1/4 cup of the heavy cream in a large glass measuring cup. When the cake has cooled, poke holes all over the surface with an ice pick or a skewer. Gradually pour all but 1 cup of the milk mixture over the top of the cake. Discard the remaining 1 cup of the milk mixture. Allow the soaked cake to sit for 25 to 30 minutes.

Beat the remaining 2 cups heavy cream at high speed in the bowl of the electric mixer, adding the powdered sugar 1 tablespoon at a time, about 3 minutes. When the cream is thick, spread over the top of the soaked cake. Serve immediately or refrigerate for later use.

Buttermilk Pralines

A trip to New Orleans is not complete without these melt-in-your-mouth nut clusters, and a trip to your home should be no different. All it takes is a good candy thermometer and a bit of stir time and you've got dessert.

YIELD: ABOUT 35 CANDIES

3 cups sugar

1 cup buttermilk

3/4 cup light corn syrup

1 teaspoon baking soda

1/8 teaspoon salt

2 cups pecan halves

1 teaspoon pure vanilla extract

1 tablespoon butter

Cover two large baking sheets with waxed paper and place on wire racks. Clip a candy thermometer to the side of a large Dutch oven over medium heat, being careful that the tip doesn't touch the bottom of the pot. Add the sugar, buttermilk, corn syrup, baking soda, and salt. Stir until the sugar dissolves and the mixture comes to a boil.

Stir constantly to the soft ball stage, or until the candy thermometer reaches 236 degrees. Remove from the heat and stir in the pecans, vanilla, and butter. Beat by hand until the candy is thick and creamy, around 3 minutes. Quickly drop by spoonsful onto the waxed paper. Allow to cool completely, then remove from the waxed paper into airtight containers until ready to serve.

NOTE: *The candy mixture will foam rapidly and rise in the pot as it begins to boil. Make sure you use a long-handled wooden spoon for stirring.*

Lemon Angel Food Cake

There is no better day to serve this dessert than Sunday. It just seems appropriate thanks to the name, and this version has just a tiny bit of a nippy tang! Use any fresh fruit that is in season as a garnish.

YIELD: 12 TO 14 SERVINGS

....

18 large egg whites, room temperature

1 teaspoon cream of tartar

2 1/2 cups sugar

1 1/2 cups all-purpose flour

1/4 teaspoon salt

1 teaspoon lemon extract

1 teaspoon lemon juice

....

Preheat the oven to 375 degrees. Grease a 10-inch tube pan.

Place the egg whites and cream of tartar in the bowl of an electric mixer. Beat at high speed with the whisk attachment until stiff peaks form, around 2 minutes. In a medium bowl stir together the sugar, flour, and salt.

Reduce the mixer speed to low and gradually fold in the sugar mixture one-third at a time, blending just until mixed after each addition. Fold in the lemon extract and lemon juice and transfer the batter to the prepared pan.

Bake 50 to 55 minutes or until the top immediately springs back when lightly touched. Invert onto a wire rack to cool completely, about 2 hours. Remove the tube pan, using a dinner knife to run around the pan edges to loosen if necessary. Transfer to a serving plate, slice, and serve.

Sunday Dinner Memories

Father Roger McDonald loves to eat. He is nearly at a loss when asked if there are foods he doesn't like, but the list is long of those he thoroughly enjoys. At the top would have to be pound cake. He loves it plain or topped, warm or cold, toasted or not, and in any flavor.

That made it easy for the cooks in his Catholic church near New Orleans to prepare treats for him, and he was grateful for the time and love that went into every food gift. "There was always pound cake for dessert when I dined with members of the church," he said, "and I never grew tired of it."

It came as no surprise when at the church's annual cake walk fund-raiser, there were over two dozen pound cakes available to win. Roger was elated at the possibilities that were prepared by some of the finest cooks in the parish. Of the forty cakes on display, twenty-six of them were pound cakes. His head was swimming with dreams of the one he would be taking home. He had his money ready and was one of the first in line to play.

To the tune of "Pop Goes the Weasel," the participants roamed the large circle, some dancing, others skipping, and still others walking. When the music stopped, Roger took his place on his number, but was not the winner. He kept paying and playing, determined to be the recipient of one of the delicious pound cakes on display.

His luck never seemed to change, and time and time again

someone else got the cake prize. Roger soon realized that the pound cakes were dwindling fast as the game continued. To his dismay, Roger never won, and he could hardly believe he was going to have to leave without anything in hand. He was trying to laugh about it, but was sincerely disappointed.

That's when Esther Carter approached him with a covered tray in hand. Each of the twenty-six winners of the pound cakes had graciously donated a slice of their prize to him for being such a good sport. And as he journeyed home, his heart was light from the thoughtfulness and heavy with the decision of which one he would try first!

Frosted Sweet Potato Cake

There are very few foods that can transition easily from appetizer to soup to side dish to dessert, but sweet potatoes can. This cake is delicately spiced and light, but flavorful at the same time. Start making it in the autumn months and you'll still be preparing it through the holidays. (Photo on page 212.)

YIELD: 12 SERVINGS

2 pounds sweet potatoes, peeled and chopped

1 3/4 cups butter, softened, divided

2 3/4 cups sugar

3 large eggs

1 teaspoon pure vanilla extract

2 cups crushed graham crackers

1 cup chopped pecans or walnuts

3 cups all-purpose flour

1 teaspoon baking soda

1 teaspoon ground cinnamon

1 teaspoon ground allspice

1 teaspoon ground nutmeg

1 teaspoon salt

1/2 teaspoon baking powder

Cream Cheese Frosting (recipe follows)

Place the potatoes in a large saucepan and cover with water. Place over medium-high heat and bring to a boil. Cook 25 minutes, drain well, and set aside to cool for 15 minutes.

Preheat the oven to 350 degrees. Grease and flour 3 (9-inch) cake pans.

In the bowl of an electric mixer, beat 1 cup of the butter and the sugar for 2 minutes until light and fluffy. Add the eggs, one at a time, beating well after each addition. Stir in the vanilla and blend well.

In a medium bowl combine the remaining 3/4 cup butter with the graham crackers and pecans. Mix well and divide evenly among the prepared pans. Press into the bottom of each pan.

In another medium bowl combine the flour, baking soda, cinnamon, allspice, nutmeg, salt, and baking powder. Add the flour mixture alternately to the butter mixture with the cooled sweet potatoes. Divide the batter among the pans and spread over the graham cracker crust.

Bake for 28 minutes or until a tester inserted in the center comes out clean. Let cool in the pans on a wire rack for 10 minutes. Turn each cake out onto a wire rack to cool completely.

Prepare the Cream Cheese Frosting and place one cake layer on a serving platter. Frost the top and add the second layer. Repeat and add the third layer using the remaining frosting. Let stand at least 1 hour before slicing and serving.

Cream Cheese Frosting

Don't just save this for Sweet Potato Cake. It's equally divine spread over chocolate cake or cupcakes.

YIELD: 4 1/2 CUPS

2 (8-ounce) packages cream
  cheese, softened
1 cup (2 sticks) butter, softened

2 teaspoons pure vanilla extract
1 (16-ounce) package powdered
  sugar

In the bowl of an electric mixer, beat together the cream cheese, butter, and vanilla at medium speed for 2 minutes. Reduce the mixer speed to low and add half of the powdered sugar, mixing well. Add the remaining powdered sugar and beat until smooth. Use to frost a completely cooled cake.

Zesty Lemon Curd Pie

Cold pie that is served on hot, humid days just seems right. And this one is easy as can be thanks to a prepared graham cracker crust that you can pick up at the supermarket.

YIELD: 8 SERVINGS

4 large eggs

1 1/2 cups sugar

1/2 cup lemon juice

1 tablespoon grated lemon zest

1/4 teaspoon salt

1/2 cup (1 stick) butter, softened

1 (9-inch) graham cracker crust

Whisk the eggs in a medium saucepan for 1 minute. Add the sugar, lemon juice, zest, and salt and whisk to combine. Place over medium heat and add the butter, whisking constantly for 7 to 10 minutes or until the mixture thickens. Immediately remove from the heat and pour into the graham cracker crust.

Let stand at room temperature to cool on a wire rack for 1 hour. Then refrigerate at least 4 hours or until ready to slice and serve.

NOTE: *Do not let the curd mixture come to a boil while cooking or it will separate.*

Sunday Dinner Memories

Somehow kids can get adults to do things they normally would never do with anyone else. It's their innocence that gets to you and turns even crusty, hardened, polished grown-ups into children themselves.

Robert Anthony prided himself on being a professional at all times. As an associate pastor of a large Presbyterian church in Atlanta, Georgia, during the 1990s, he was a respected member of the clergy who was also a leader in the community.

A growing church demands increasing amounts of time, and while others on staff occasionally had difficulty juggling the work load, Robert flowed through the days seamlessly. At least he did until he missed a step on the way out of church one day and fell, breaking his ankle.

The cast and crutches were a struggle. When therapy started, he grumbled at the twice-a-week trips to continue his healing. He didn't realize it at the time, but he was angry at himself for the accident and the resulting disruption to his carefully planned work schedule.

At the therapy center, Robert found himself on the same schedule as a lady named Rachel who was in a strikingly similar physical situation. She had a young son named Mickey who looked to be around four years old. He usually sat quietly for most of the therapy sessions and colored or played with some building blocks.

Sometimes, if Robert finished before Mickey's mom, he would sit with him and play. As the therapy continued, Robert found himself looking forward to the stolen moments he spent with Mickey. He actually enjoyed being around this interesting little guy more and more.

One day it was obvious the staff at the center had planned some sort of birthday celebration because there were all sorts of goodies stacked in the corner. As usual, when he finished his own therapy, Robert went over to where Mickey was and they colored. Mickey asked if he would like a cookie. Robert said sure, and Mickey whipped out a few cream-filled chocolate sandwich cookies from his backpack. They gobbled down the cookies, and then, to Robert's surprise, Mickey produced even more cookies. By this time, they had the giggles and just kept eating cookie after cookie, enjoying themselves enormously.

Rachel finished her therapy and came to retrieve Mickey just after the last of their cookie supply was eliminated. She gathered their things, thanked Robert for his kindness, and left. Robert went to the desk to schedule his next appointment, not realizing that his teeth were filled with chocolate cookie bits. He talked to all the staff as he normally did, then went to the bank, and finally the cleaners. He didn't see the mess in his teeth until he got home. It made him laugh that no one said a word.

At his next appointment, he was disappointed to find out that Rachel's therapy was complete. As he was walking back for his final session, he overheard one of the staff members say, "That's the preacher who stole our cookies!" and he laughed again. When he got ready to leave, he left some money on the counter with a note that said, "Never be afraid to eat cookies with a child. Thanks for the lesson in not taking myself too seriously."

Patti's Honeybell Pound Cake

My friend Patti gave me this recipe along with some scrumptious Florida Honeybell oranges one year for Christmas. It instantly hooked me, and while you can substitute other orange varieties for it in the recipe, there is nothing like the honey sweetness it adds to this moist pound cake.

YIELD: 10 SERVINGS

1 (18.25-ounce) package lemon cake mix

1 (3-ounce) package orange gelatin

4 large eggs

3/4 cup plus 1/3 cup Honeybell or orange juice, divided

1/2 cup vegetable or canola oil

3 tablespoons grated Honeybell or orange zest, divided

2 cups powdered sugar

2 tablespoons butter, melted

Preheat the oven to 300 degrees. Grease and flour a 10-inch Bundt pan.

In the bowl of an electric mixer, combine the cake mix, gelatin, eggs, 3/4 cup of the juice, oil, and 1 tablespoon of the zest. Mix at medium-high speed until well blended, about 2 minutes. Transfer the batter to the prepared Bundt pan. Bake for 1 hour and 15 minutes or until a tester inserted in the center comes out clean. Cool the cake in the pan for 5 minutes, then transfer to a wire rack to cool for 10 minutes.

In a medium bowl whisk together the powdered sugar, melted butter, and the remaining 1/3 cup juice and 2 tablespoons zest. When the cake has cooled but is still warm, transfer to a serving plate and poke holes in the top of the cake with a skewer. Slowly drizzle the cake with the glaze. Cool completely before slicing and serving.

Chocolate Cobbler

My mother gave me this recipe, and it is so delicious and easy. In fact, it's so easy you can get it ready and place it in the oven while you sit down for dinner. Just as you finish, the intoxicating aroma will remind you that something fabulous is on the way.

YIELD: 8 TO 10 SERVINGS

1 cup (2 sticks) butter

1 1/2 cups self-rising flour

2 1/2 cups sugar, divided

3/4 cup milk

1 tablespoon pure vanilla extract

6 tablespoons unsweetened cocoa

2 cups water

Vanilla ice cream

Place the butter in a 9 x 13-inch baking dish and let it melt in the oven while it pre-heats to 350 degrees. In a medium bowl combine the flour, 1 1/2 cups of the sugar, milk, and vanilla until well blended. In a small bowl combine the remaining 1 cup sugar and cocoa.

When the butter has completely melted, remove the dish from the oven and pour the flour mixture over the top. Do not stir. Sprinkle the cocoa mixture over the top. Gradually pour the water over the top. Do not stir. Bake for 35 to 40 minutes or until lightly browned. Let stand 5 minutes before serving warm with vanilla ice cream.

Sweet Potato Pecan Pie

I dearly love sweet potatoes as a side dish, but when you place mashed ones in a piecrust, something magical happens. This version is from my mother and is enhanced with pecan halves. In the hour that it bakes, your house is going to smell terrific!

YIELD: 8 SERVINGS

1 Food Processor Piecrust
  (page 227)
1 tablespoon powdered sugar
4 large eggs
1 1/2 cups firmly packed brown
  sugar*
1 cup cooked and mashed sweet
  potatoes

1/2 cup corn syrup
1/2 cup (1 stick) butter, melted
2 tablespoons all-purpose flour
2 tablespoons milk
2 teaspoons pure vanilla extract
1 1/2 cups pecan halves

Preheat the oven to 350 degrees. Place the piecrust in a 10-inch pie plate and sprinkle the bottom with the powdered sugar.

In a medium bowl whisk the eggs and add the brown sugar, sweet potatoes, corn syrup, melted butter, flour, milk, and vanilla. Mix well and spoon into the piecrust. Top with the pecan halves. Bake for 30 minutes, then reduce the oven temperature to 300 degrees. Bake for 30 minutes longer and transfer to a wire rack to cool completely. Serve slightly warm or at room temperature.

* You can use either light or dark brown sugar for this recipe.

Caramel Fudge

This candy provides just the right amount of sweet to end a meal. This old-fashioned favorite is easy to do ahead as long as you have a good candy thermometer.

YIELD: 3 POUNDS

....

1 1/2 cups white sugar
1 1/2 cups firmly packed light
   brown sugar
1/2 cup heavy cream

1/4 cup light corn syrup
1/4 cup water
1 teaspoon pure vanilla extract
1 cup chopped pecans

....

In a heavy saucepan over medium heat, combine the white sugar, brown sugar, heavy cream, corn syrup, and water. Stir until the sugars dissolve and the mixture begins to boil. Reduce the heat to medium-low. Cover and cook 2 minutes. Uncover and attach a candy thermometer to the saucepan, making sure the tip doesn't touch the bottom of the pan. Cook without stirring until the mixture reaches 242 degrees.

Remove from the heat and cool about 1 hour to 110 degrees. Grease an 8- or 9-inch square baking pan. Stir in the vanilla and beat by hand until the candy loses its gloss and becomes creamy, about 4 minutes. Stir in the pecans and transfer to the prepared pan. Cool completely before cutting into squares. Store in an airtight container.

Beverages

Peach-Infused Tea

This tea recipe calls for fresh peaches, but works equally well with farm-fresh nectarines or apricots. I like the version sweetened with agave nectar best. You'll find it bottled and sold in the baking aisle of the supermarket.

YIELD: 8 SERVINGS

7 cups water

8 peach-flavored regular-size tea bags

2/3 cup agave nectar (see sugar substitute below)

2 cups peeled and sliced fresh peaches

Place the water in a large saucepan over high heat. Bring to a boil and remove the pan from the heat. Add the tea bags and steep for 6 minutes. Remove and squeeze the tea bags, then discard. Add the agave nectar to the steeped tea and stir well to combine.

Place the fresh peaches in a pitcher and add the tea. Cover and refrigerate. Serve cold over ice.

SUGAR SUBSTITUTE: *While the tea steeps, place a cup of water and 1 cup of sugar in a small saucepan over medium-high heat. Bring to a simmer and immediately remove from the heat. Stir to dissolve the sugar and add to the tea.*

Fresh Blackberry Iced Tea

Adding fresh summer fruit to ordinary brewed tea takes it up a notch to make your guests feel extra special. Freeze portions of this in ice-cube trays so it will not be diluted by water as the ice melts.

Yield: 6 servings

4 cups fresh blackberries

8 1/4 cups water, divided

6 regular-size tea bags or 2
   family-size tea bags

2/3 cup sugar

Fresh mint sprigs for garnish

Place the blackberries and 1/4 cup of the water in a medium saucepan over high heat. Bring to a boil and reduce the heat to low. Simmer 3 minutes and remove from the heat. Set aside to cool slightly.

Place 4 cups of the remaining water in a large saucepan over high heat. Bring to a boil and remove the pan from the heat. Add the tea bags and sugar, stirring well. Allow to steep for 6 minutes. Remove and squeeze the tea bags, then discard. Stir in the remaining 4 cups water.

Strain the blackberry mixture into the tea using a fine-mesh sieve. Press the berries with the back of a wooden spoon to extract as much juice as possible. Discard the solids. Transfer to a tea pitcher, cover, and refrigerate until ready to serve. Serve cold over ice with a garnish of mint.

SUNDAY DINNER MEMORIES

Bill Reasoner gives new meaning to the word *tea-totaler*. He loves ice-cold sweet tea, and at eighty-seven years old, he consumes it by the pitcherful on a daily basis. Tall glasses of iced tea have gotten him through seminary, then through literally hundreds of visits with the sick and elderly.

As a retired minister, it still cools him off during the sticky hot springs, summers, and falls common in south Alabama. In his words, "I don't drink coffee, juice, soft drinks, liquor, or beer . . . just tea!"

He is quite the tea connoisseur and likes it sweetened with real sugar and doesn't add lemon. When the ice cubes start to water the elixir down, he's ready for another glass. This man loves his tea, and his congregation knew it.

About ten years ago, Bill was invited to have dinner after church with Bobby and Sue Russell, and it was life changing. While he doesn't remember a thing about what they ate, he distinctly remembers the tea. Sue served it in extra-large dark-blue glasses, and it was sweetened to perfection, just the way Bill liked it. As he drank the tea with the meal, the ice clanked happily in the glass. He knew it would soon start to water down from the melting ice, and he dreaded that because the tea was so good.

As the meal continued, Bill was surprised that the tea never tasted diluted, even though they lingered into the afternoon at the table. Finally, as he was getting ready to leave, he commented on how nice the meal was and how much he especially enjoyed the tea. That's when Sue told him she froze prepared tea in ice cube trays to make the ice so that the beverage would stay fresh throughout the meal.

"I have done the same thing since that meal and whisper thanks to her every time I pour the tea into the trays," he told me. Little acts of kindness and forethought make a big difference, and Sue's idea has made the beverage in Bill's glass "tea-rific!"

Cucumber Water with Lemon

Flavored water is nothing short of refreshing. It goes well with salads or before a meal. On hot summer days, you'll find this beverage cools you off quickly.

YIELD: 6 TO 8 SERVINGS

....

2 quarts water   1 small lemon
1 medium cucumber

....

Place the water in a large pitcher. Using a zester, peel strips of the outer skin every inch lengthwise across the cucumber. Remove and discard the ends and cut into large wedges. Add to the water. Cover and refrigerate for 2 hours.

Cut the lemon into 6 slices and add to the cucumber water. Cover and refrigerate 2 hours longer or up to 6 hours. Serve cold over ice.

Mixed Berry and Citrus Sparkling Tea

Club soda is my pick for this sparkling tea, but if you want to have it sweeter, use either ginger ale or lemon–lime soda.

Yield: 8 servings

2 cups water

4 regular-size tea bags

1 1/2 cups mixed berries
   (raspberries, seedless
   blackberries, blueberries)

1 cup lemon or orange juice

2 cups chilled club soda, lemon-
   lime soda, or ginger ale

Place the water and tea bags in a small saucepan over high heat and bring to a boil. Remove from the heat and allow to steep for 6 minutes.

Place the berries and juice in the bowl of a food processor or blender. Process until smooth and transfer to a serving pitcher.

Squeeze and discard the tea bags and stir the tea into the fruit mixture in the serving pitcher. Cover and chill for at least 1 hour. When ready to serve, stir in the club soda and pour into ice-filled glasses.

NOTE: *For a sweeter tea, add 1/4 cup of agave nectar to the mixture before refrigerating.*

Raspberry Iced Tea

Raspberries can be a bit difficult for some to enjoy because of the tiny seeds. This recipe eliminates that problem deliciously.

Yield: 6 servings

4 cups fresh raspberries

8 cups water, divided

6 regular-size tea bags or 2 family-size tea bags

3/4 cup sugar

Lemon slices for garnish

Place the raspberries and 1 cup of the water in a medium saucepan over high heat. Bring to a boil and reduce the heat to low. Simmer 3 minutes and remove from the heat. Set aside to cool slightly.

Place 4 cups of the remaining water in a large saucepan over high heat. Bring to a boil and remove from the heat. Add the tea bags and sugar, stirring well. Allow to steep for 6 minutes. Remove and squeeze the tea bags, then discard. Stir in the remaining 3 cups water.

Strain the raspberry mixture into the tea using a fine-mesh sieve. Press the berries with the back of a wooden spoon to extract as much juice as possible. Discard the solids. Transfer to a tea pitcher, cover, and refrigerate until ready to serve. Serve cold over ice with lemon slices for garnish.

Basil Lime Spritzer

This beverage is light and instantly refreshing without killing your appetite for the upcoming dinner. Serve it to guests sitting on the front porch while you get the meal on the table. It should be made ahead of time and thoroughly chilled.

YIELD: 8 SERVINGS

3/4 cup sugar

Zest strips of 1 lime

1/2 cup lime juice

1/2 cup water

3/4 cup loosely packed fresh basil

Sparkling water

Lime slices

In a medium saucepan over medium-high heat, combine the sugar, zest, lime juice, and water. Stir until the sugar has dissolved and bring to a boil. Immediately remove the pan from the heat and let the mixture stand for 20 minutes to cool.

With a slotted spoon, remove and discard the zest. Transfer to a blender container and add the basil. Blend for 15 seconds. Pour through a fine-mesh sieve lined with a coffee filter into a small bowl. Let cool completely and refrigerate.

When ready to serve, pour 2 tablespoons of the syrup into 8 tall (at least 8-ounce) ice-filled glasses. Add sparkling water and garnish with lime slices. Serve immediately.

Pink Lemonade

Lemonade is such a nice blend of sweetness and tang, and this pink version is a great variation of ordinary recipes thanks to a sugar syrup. It should be served in tall, ice-filled glasses on front porches in the summertime.

YIELD: ABOUT 3 QUARTS

1 cup water

3 1/2 cups sugar, divided

2 1/2 cups lemon juice

2 cups cranberry juice cocktail

In a small saucepan over medium-high heat, combine the water and 1 cup of the sugar. Bring to a boil, stirring to completely dissolve the sugar. Remove from the heat and cool completely.

Place the remaining 2 1/2 cups sugar in the bowl of a food processor. Process for 10 seconds and transfer to a serving pitcher. Add the lemon and cranberry juices and stir to blend. Add the cooled sugar syrup and stir well. Refrigerate until ready to serve over ice.

Cantaloupe Coolers

Fresh cantaloupe is now in your glass, and deliciously I might add. It works equally well with honeydew that you have picked up at the farmers' market.

YIELD: 8 SERVINGS

1 (4-pound) cantaloupe, peeled, seeded, and cut into cubes

1 1/2 cups water, divided

1 tablespoon sugar

1 tablespoon lime juice

1/8 teaspoon salt

1 quart chilled soda water

Lime slices for garnish

Line a large colander with fine-mesh cheesecloth and place over a deep bowl. Puree half of the cantaloupe and 3/4 cup water in a blender. Transfer to the colander and repeat with the remaining cantaloupe and 3/4 cup water. Allow to drain for 1 hour at room temperature. Gather the cheesecloth and gently squeeze any remaining juice from the melon. Discard the solids.

Stir in the sugar, lime juice, and salt. Cover and refrigerate at least 1 hour. Divide the cantaloupe mixture among 8 tall (at least 8-ounce) ice-filled glasses. Top off with soda water and garnish with lime slices. Serve immediately.

SUNDAY DINNER MEMORIES

The words *aroma* and *smell* are similar, but can be worlds apart in what they mean. We generally use *aroma* to describe something pleasant. The word *smell*, on the other hand, tends to denote a more distasteful odor.

John Griffin pulls those two words out when he talks about a food experience that stands above the rest. John grew up in the Catholic church, and as a child, he greatly anticipated the incense as it wafted through the pews. He always associated that scent with holiness and looked forward to having it fill his nostrils.

But just like many things, that enthusiasm waned as he matured, and he didn't pay as much attention to the sweet fragrance when he entered the ministry. It took a trip to the local coffee shop to bring it back.

John liked walking and made it a point to get out and "roam the streets" of his parish in Louisiana as frequently as possible. With no particular mission in mind, he would drive to an area, park, then get out and start walking. The experience always found a way to bless him, no matter the time of year.

On a still, rather chilly and misty spring day, he was making a trek when he spotted a coffee shop in the distance. Thinking a hot drink was just what he needed to warm up, he headed in that direction. Not a big coffee drinker, he was looking more forward to holding the hot beverage than drinking it. He ordered, paid, and decided it might be nice to sit inside at one of the stools positioned to look out the front windows for a bit.

He hadn't been sitting there long when an elderly gentleman sidled up next to him at the window. He instantly started whistling a happy tune, and John commented on his cheerful spirit. The man immediately launched into a dialogue on how glorious the day was and that he wished every day was this spectacular. John couldn't help but ask what made this day so exceptional.

The man held up his coffee cup and asked John to drink in the aroma from his own cup. "Do you smell that?" the man asked. "It is home! I am home after being gone for nearly two years. Can you imagine a fragrance sweeter than the smell of home?" he continued.

Then the man turned and left as quickly as he appeared, going his merry way and whistling as he made his way down the street. "It made me smile, and suddenly I was enjoying that cup of coffee as I never had before," he said. The experience has stayed with him to this day, along with a renewed appreciation for the ordinary. And when he smells the incense at church now, he smiles and thanks God for the delicious aroma of home.

Iced Coffee

Southerners are always looking for ways to cool off during our steamy summers, which seem to command more months than the other seasons. Iced coffee is a terrific way to end a meal, especially if you want to do so out on the patio.

Yield: 8 servings

1/3 cup ground coffee

4 cups water

1/2 cup flavored coffee creamer

1/4 cup sugar

Ice cubes

In a coffeemaker, brew the coffee with the water. Note that this will be stronger than regular coffee. Transfer to a large container with a lid. Stir in the creamer and sugar until the sugar completely dissolves. Add around 18 ice cubes and cover the container tightly. Shake well to chill down the coffee. Serve immediately over additional ice cubes.

About the Author

Tammy Algood is a food personality on Nashville's local ABC, CBS, NBC, and Fox affiliates, as well as statewide on PBS. You can hear her food reports and commentary on Nashville radio networks, Clear Channel, and NPR. She conducts cooking schools at various Tennessee wineries and has been published in numerous magazines and newspapers. She is the author of *Farm Fresh Southern Cooking, In a Snap!*, and *The Southern Slow Cooker Bible*.

Index